# BLOCKCHAIN
## The Hype-Free Guide

by Pauli Olavi Ojala and Sydney Rose

Illustrations by
Gahmeur H.

RoseDog Books
PITTSBURGH, PENNSYLVANIA 15238

RoseDog Books
585 Alpha Drive, Suite 103
Pittsburgh, PA 15238
Visit our website at www.rosedogbookstore.com

ISBN: 978-1-64913-057-0
eISBN: 978-1-64913-072-3

# BLOCKCHAIN
## The Hype-Free Guide

# Table of Contents

# Authors' Foreword

*From Pauli:*

This book is intended for anyone who would like to understand blockchains and related concepts from the ground up. The need for such a book became clear when I researched blockchain- and cryptocurrency-related literature in the fall of 2017. A sudden influx of money from ordinary retail investors was flowing into initial coin offerings (ICOs), and the price of Bitcoin was reaching new, vertiginous heights almost every day. Yet few people seemed to understand, or even care about, the capabilities and intrinsic limitations of the technology. A lot of what passed for expert discussion was either philosophical debate around blockchain utopias far removed from current reality, or simply someone trying to get their shady payday by shilling for one coin or another.

It was hard to find balance in the conversation. Blockchain evangelists faced off with fierce skeptics. While outnumbered by starry-eyed visionaries, the sceptics had some powerful technical arguments on their side and could point to a rapidly growing track record of failures and deception over the years.

In my decades of experience in the software industry, I've seen the repetition of hype cycles; technologies get pumped up by corporations, then abandoned a few years later. Yet there was something very different about the mood this time, as opinions were polarized in a way that is rare in the technology business where any uncertainty typically gets resolved by the marketplace in relatively short order. Even the most formidable adversaries, like Apple and Microsoft, tend to eventually settle into a mutually beneficial coexistence. No such friendly truce is on the horizon for cryptocurrencies. There are thought-provoking ideas at the core of the blockchain vision, and there are also undeniable problems with the way things are implemented and marketed. My hope is that reading this book will give you a grounded understanding that will help you apply rational judgment to the promises and opportunities in this field. [1]

We considered calling this book "Refineries of Trust." Although that didn't become the final title because it's a bit too cryptic, I'd like to use it here to explain two ideas that I believe are fundamental to this book. The first is related to the function of the blockchain. Blockchains have a core ingredient: trust. It is a human concept that describes relationships between people, and that technologists long to distill into something that can be established in code: quantifiable, verifiable, immutable. An oil refinery takes the unwieldy material of crude oil and turns it into dense, efficient fuels that power entire economies built around this easily transportable form of energy. In this limited analogy, a blockchain is the refinery that takes the raw materials—digital data, computing power, human aims, and ambitions—and attempts to condense those into an economical "digital fuel" that could offer the right combination of incentives, and digital storage characteristics to power new economies.

The other meaning of "Refineries of Trust" deals with the more social aspect of trust. ICOs have taught us again just how easy it can be to mislead and defraud the public. Extraordinary promises require extraordinary evidence, but in the case of ICOs, many buyers have been willing to accept the exorbitant trading prices of Bitcoin and Ethereum as evidence that any blockchain-based project is destined for success. There is an abundance of trust combined with a shortage of sophistication. In this way, ICOs are a Darwinist kind of trust refinery for the digital social sphere: while regulation is catching up, the would-be investor or enthusiast needs to become smarter. *Caveat creditor.*

*-Pauli Olavi Ojala*

---

[1] *If you want to complement this book with arguments from the skeptical side, you can't do better than "Attack of the 50 Foot Blockchain" by David Gerard (2017). As for the opposing faction of ultra-optimists, I hesitate to recommend specific work because authors in this space are so prolific. If you go to Medium.com and read some of the top-voted posts for topics like "cryptocurrency" and "blockchain," you'll get a solid overview of the highly optimistic position.*

## *From the Authors:*

You may have read about questionable or downright illegal activity that is increasingly being investigated by regulators around the world: ICOs that turned out to be outright scams, "pump and dump" schemes, market manipulation at exchanges, and so on. Even those who seem to be offering impartial help may have vested interests. When it comes to anything you read on the Internet, it's more important than ever to understand both the source and the motivations behind the advice.

The authors of this book want to give you a clear pledge that **this book exists for your benefit only**. There is no secondary agenda. We're not looking to promote any specific platforms or coins. To hold to this pledge, the signed authors have divested of coin and token holdings, except for small amounts necessary to test deployments and other technical aspects. We take this responsibility very seriously. You deserve better than compromised advice.

Additionally, it needs to be stated clearly that the authors are not lawyers and that the contents of this guide should not be considered as legal, accounting, tax, or official investing advice in the United States or any other jurisdiction. This book is provided as a resource, so you can feel more confident in making decisions; however, note that there are risks inherent in cryptocurrency investments, as with any investment.

Despite these warnings, we hope your primary takeaway from this book will be one of optimism about potential new ways to use the amazing global digital network that mankind has built over the past 40 years. Today's blockchains are just a starting point towards decentralized applications. Some of the platforms currently in use may succeed in retaining their value long-term, while many others will become nothing more than footnotes in technology history—such is the nature of technological evolution.

It's going to be an interesting journey once again.

*-Sydney Rose and Pauli Olavi Ojala*

# 1.

# The Blockchain Primer
# that George Washington Would Understand

Blockchains. Decentralized protocols. Distributed ledgers. Cryptographic hash functions. Consensus algorithms. The sheer amount of terminology can be daunting to the cryptocurrency newcomer. Not only are you trying to familiarize yourself with some of the more mind-bending concepts in computer science, but you also have to deal with a great dose of economics jargon.

## *Pop quiz:*

When you hear the word "fiat," is your first thought:

- A) An affordable Italian car,
- B) Federal Reserve, or
- C) a total blank?

Don't worry if it's C! By the end of this book, you'll be fluent enough that you won't be confused even when buying a Fiat with cash.

Blockchains are bringing together two opposites of the scientific mindset, which may initially seem to be at odds with each other. On one side of the ring, we have the extreme unforgiving rigor of cryptography: a math-heavy branch of computer science that used to be the exclusive domain of dusty academics. At the other side of the ring stands the brash superstar of social sciences, the economist: ready to pounce, competitive, possessing what some would describe as an abrasive personality. In this situation, however, opposites attract! When two such discrete sciences meet, there is unique opportunity in the air—but also ample room for misunderstanding and misdirection by bad actors.

So what is it that makes the blockchain unique? A marriage of economics and cryptography, okay—but is it all just about a technological solution? If you read online discussions, you may find that most participants are very caught up in heated debate involving the merit of exceptionally specific details of blockchain implementations. Getting the big picture is not easy.

Fundamentally, the most important part of blockchains is not algorithms, nor cloud servers, nor user interfaces—it's people. More specifically: it's about **accountability between people**. This is a concept that is closely related to trust, yet narrower because trust comes in so many forms. For example, trust in a marriage is something that typically is not built on task accountability—your wife, husband, or partner doesn't expect you to file precise reports of everything you did during an average day. Hence marital trust is not something that seems very amenable to a blockchain-based solution, or a technology solution in general. Of course, if you think you have a viable project concept here, disregard this example, and go for it! The market would certainly be enormous.

Accountability has sparked financial revolutions before. The modern accounting system of double-entry bookkeeping was widely adopted in Italy in the 13th century, and it became a crucial foundation of the creative and economic boom in Western Europe during the Renaissance. In Florence, a man named Giovanni de' Medici founded a bank on the rigorous principles of the double-entry bookkeeping system. His son, Cosimo, became the ruler of Florence, and three generations later, one of Cosimo's great-grandsons became Pope Leo X, the highest office in Europe at the time. This is pretty good for a dynasty built primarily on Giovanni's astute understanding of an accounting innovation!

Most applications of modern information technology in corporations are evolved descendants of the medieval Medici Bank's operations: maintaining databases, recording transactions, and storing the details of who did what and how other accounts were affected. In accounting terms, these systems are **ledgers**. How is a blockchain different from what goes on in a corporation's IT systems already? How does a blockchain enable new forms of accountability between people?

The keyword is decentralization. Whichever previous system you consider—the Medicis' handwritten ledgers stored in volumes of books, a present-day bank's IBM mainframe, or even the cluster of replicated cloud servers you might find at a more forward-looking corporation today—you'll discover that there is a single source of truth. Someone is authorized to perform operations on the accounts, and that "truth" is stored in all copies of the information. No matter how many cloud servers are used to provide resilience in case a system goes down, inputs to the system are centralized—there's ultimately an authority that says, "This data comes from a reliable source, it's approved to be recorded in our system."

The blockchain is not like those traditional ledgers with a single input for truth. It is a **distributed ledger**—a term you will hear often in blockchain discussions. When there are multiple inputs, a single gatekeeper can't decide what truth "sticks" in the permanent ledger, so there is the need for **consensus**—another term that you'll encounter frequently.

To better understand distributed ledgers and consensus, let's step back entirely from the context of computers and digital systems, and look at a historical example. Imagine yourself in New York in 1750! You've just stepped off a ship that brought you all the way from London, a three-week journey across the Atlantic. Rough seas, bad food, foul-smelling passengers—you're happy to be back on solid ground.

As it happens, you are a rich man. In your pocket, you have a bill of considerable value: a money order for 1,000 pounds from one of the most respected banks in London. The bank's name is well-known, even in the most remote English colonies, and your note carries the official stamp of their London branch. In New York, you immediately seek out a wealthy trader whose company has a formal association with the London bank. The bank provides the trader with a credit line back in England, and in exchange, the trader has made a pledge that he will accept the bank's money orders in New York and cash them out.

The trader never expected someone with your kind of wealth to walk in with a money order in hand, though. Cash is scarce in the colonies. The trader keeps perhaps 50 pounds' worth of gold in his office. Cashing out a thousand-pound money order is an operation that will take weeks, or even months, to execute. He'd very much like you to just go away and take your money order somewhere else, but he's bound by the contract made with the London bank.

How does this turn out? How can the trader know whether your money order is valid? How can you prove its validity despite the trader's obvious desire to not give you the cash? It's a scenario that asks core questions about accountability between people. By the way, it is also the plot of the novel *Golden Hill* by Francis Spufford. If you like the concept, check it out!

At the bank in London, there is a ledger that proves your account contains a thousand pounds. The trader doesn't have a copy of those books, though, and requesting proof across the Atlantic will take months. How does one distribute the information in that ledger without having to send letters back and forth at every request? There are two ways.

First, you could send the same information through multiple routes. In fact, this is what the bank and the trader have agreed to do. For any money order, the bank will send a second copy of the bill on another ship, entrusted to the ship's captain personally. When (or if) the second ship arrives and the captain appears at the trader's office to vouch for your bill with another stamped copy in hand, the trader will most likely accept its authenticity. In that case, consensus has been achieved.

Another way to distribute the ledger would be to send **cryptographically verified** bills. This was feasible—though admittedly not common practice—even with 18th century technology. The bank and the trader could have shared a code book when they originally met in London. Using the code book, the bank would insert a message into your money order that could only be decoded by someone who has a copy of the code book.

The problem with this approach is that you'd have to trust the trader when it comes to the verification of the money order. He doesn't really want to pay you the thousand pounds, so even if your order's coded message verifies, what's stopping him from lying to you about it?

Ideally, you'd have both. The bank would use cryptography to make their money orders verifiable by the recipient, and they would also use consensus by sending a copy of the data by a trusted party—in this case, the second ship's captain who was paid by the bank to lend his authority to the order's copy.

Flash forward 250 years. It doesn't take two months to send a message and get a reply across the Atlantic anymore, but the problems of sharing ledgers and trusting accounts haven't gone away. Now that the process of sending messages is nearly instantaneous, even across oceans; the issue is the great number of participants, all busy with various trades. Our 1750 scenario had just four people—you, the bank, the trader, and the second ship's captain. The trader received only a handful of money orders a month, so he could dedicate time to resolving the transaction. Today, we have billions of people each doing potentially hundreds of transactions daily. Who are the gatekeepers of all this? Who owns the ledgers and decides who gets an account in them? Who decides that, say, someone in a particular country is disenfranchised, forbidden from participating in the global financial system due to political events that took place before the person was even born? What kind of alternative systems could we build without the previous set of assumptions?

The blockchain allows an opportunity to explore those questions outside the structure of the established systems that have a single source of truth. It combines two features we've already seen in the 1750 scenario—consensus and cryptographic verification—and puts them together in a novel way to create a truly decentralized system where multiple actors can be sources of truth, and they have shared incentives to arrive at a single truth which then gets permanently recorded by everyone. Those "truths" are stored in uniquely identified blocks, and the permanent, mutually agreed record is a "chain" where every block points to the previous one, so the order can't be tampered with—hence, **blockchain**.

Although our examples so far have dealt with transferring money, remember that this is really about accountability between people. The accounts and values represented on the distributed ledger do not necessarily need to represent a currency transaction. They can be created in basically any situation where one party (or several) acknowledges a fact about another party on the network.

In practice, the facts you'd want to store on a blockchain divide primarily into two categories: **ownership** and **promises**. What exactly a particular blockchain supports depends on its **protocol**.

The first widely deployed blockchains concerned themselves only with a single type of value or asset: the accounts containing those values, and the records of transactions between those accounts. Bitcoin is the flagship example of this type of "value-store" blockchain. To put it another way, the Bitcoin protocol doesn't let you do anything with your account's Bitcoin balance except transfer it to another account. The Bitcoin ledger records ownership, and that's it.

There are many other blockchain protocols that are concerned with the second category mentioned above that we called "promises." Think of a simple non-monetary exchange: maybe you buy us coffee, and we promise to clean your apartment later. (We're desperate for coffee!) That's not exactly ownership; you don't own a cleaned apartment, but it is a promise that could be stored on the blockchain, so that you could hold us to it. These kinds of simple promises are often **tokenized**; that is, turned into an asset category that can be traded and owned on the blockchain. If we gave you the same promise in the form of a generic "apartment-cleaning token," you could then sell it to, or trade it with, someone else on the blockchain, and we'd have an undeniable agreement that we are now obligated to clean the apartment of that third person instead.

An advanced form of promises is called **smart contracts**. With these, you can essentially ask the blockchain deep questions and hold the participants accountable to some behavior that is automatically applied by the blockchain itself. For example, we could promise to clean apartments for the first 10 people who buy us coffee today. Our "apartment-cleaning token creator" smart contract would be executed to generate up to 10 tokens—but no more than 10, and only today. Those limits are enforced by the smart contract definition, which is automatically processed by the blockchain participants. Since the smart contract is encoded on the blockchain, the rules are visible to all and cannot be changed, so we can't later decide to make changes unilaterally even if we wanted to get out of this promise to clean 10 apartments.

There is also a special kind of ownership that can be represented on a blockchain that links other kinds of digital data into the blockchain's world of cryptographic truths. It revolves around the concept of a **hash value**, which will be explained in further detail later. For now, it's enough to say that a "hash" is a short fingerprint value, represented by a short sequence of numbers that is guaranteed to be unique, which can be computed for any kind of digital content. You could take this book and calculate its hash, or an entire Windows install disk, or a digitized copy of a Beatles album—all these, and anything else in digital form, can be condensed down into a single hash. Hashes are "one-way": you can't reconstruct the data from the hash, nor can you come up with invented data that would fit a particular hash.

This latter property of hashes turns out to be very useful. By computing a hash and publishing it, you can prove the existence of some data right now, without exposing any potentially proprietary details, so that you can refer to this record of the data later. A patent makes a great example because there could be legal disputes regarding who invented something first. When you're preparing to file for a patent, you could save a draft explaining the invention and publish that text's hash on a blockchain. If there is ever a dispute later, you'd be able to prove your invention date by publishing the draft text and showing that it matches the hash that remains stored on the blockchain. It's not possible to forge a text later that would match the hash, so this is solid proof that you had the invention written down when the hash was published.

Hashes are extremely important to how many aspects of blockchains are implemented, so you'll encounter the term in many contexts. We'll clarify the various uses of hashes later. For now, just remember that creating digital fingerprints of content is one very practical application of **hashing** when considering how your own blockchain protocol will work.

Remember how we said earlier that the Bitcoin ledger just records ownership of the coins created on the network? Strictly speaking there is a "loophole" in the Bitcoin protocol for tucking small amounts of other data within transactions, and this loophole is just large enough to put a hash value there. So, you could even use the Bitcoin blockchain to save your digital ownership fingerprints. It is worth noting that you'd pay the Bitcoin transaction fee each time, which at the time of writing, is currently equal to about $0.30 USD.

In practice, you'd be better off using a different protocol, specifically one that's explicitly designed to store this kind of data more cheaply and efficiently. Still, this Bitcoin transaction loophole is an illustrative example of how a blockchain really is just a shared record of facts, and those facts can be anything that the protocol lets you store and access.

There are two features that are commonly associated with blockchains, yet they are actually implementation choices and not inherently required by the concept. They are **mining** and **anonymity**. Maybe you've seen stories in the press about how Bitcoin mining now consumes more energy than the entire country of Denmark, or how Ethereum mining has fueled such demand for high-end graphics processing units (GPUs) that for some time it was nearly impossible to buy a graphics card for your gaming PC[2]. These are highly visible side effects of a choice that was made by the Bitcoin and Ethereum blockchain protocol designers. They both acquire consensus through "mining," which means that blockchain participants will have their computers perform complex computations that are useless in and of themselves but verifiable by others, all while processing transactions, and for that work, they get rewarded with coins on the blockchain.

This kind of consensus-building is called ***Proof of Work (PoW)***. It's a very clever way to ensure that a blockchain with an arbitrary number of participants who don't know each other can still reach consensus. As long as there's not a single party doing more than 50 percent of the mining, this approach guarantees fairness. Its downside is energy consumption due to the work that is useless in itself since none of those computations have any meaning other than verifying transactions. There are other approaches, in particular **Proof of Stake (PoS)**. We'll discuss these approaches in later chapters. For now, to get better understanding of the issue, let's quickly refer back to the 1750 scenario: what kind of consensus was used there? The second ship's captain provided a copy of the money order and vouched for its authenticity on his honor, so we could call this approach **Proof of Authority**. It's an illustrative example of an "old world" way of solving the same problem, but the whole point of blockchains is to be independent of centralized authorities, so we don't commonly see Proof of Authority used there.

The other feature mentioned above, often associated with blockchains but not inherently required, is anonymity. Accountability between people is independent of whether those people can identify each other. Some blockchains are explicitly designed to hide participants' real-world identities, which can be useful for a wide range of things, from avoiding state censorship to selling illegal drugs. Others are explicitly designed to provide verified personal identities, such as for storing real estate deals on the blockchain. Most blockchain protocols actually fall somewhere

---

[2]  Demand has subsided since the headiest days of 2018, to the great relief of PC gaming enthusiasts.

in the middle on the anonymity spectrum. For example, Bitcoin seems anonymous on the surface, but tracing transactions back to real identities is often not as difficult as it appears. In other words, you probably shouldn't count on the IRS or your local tax office being totally ignorant of Bitcoin sales.

This concludes the high-level overview of what blockchains do, but we haven't yet touched on "how" they work more than superficially. In the next chapter we'll design a simple blockchain from scratch, then explore the underlying concepts in further detail and dive into practical applications of tokens and the design of protocols to support them.

# 2.

# Protocols, Nodes, Keys, Tokens, Coins—Explained from First Principles

Typically, a detailed explanation of how cryptocurrencies work would start by describing Bitcoin, the progenitor and esteemed great-grandmother of the hundreds of coins and tokens that have sprung up in recent years. The problem with that approach is that understanding Bitcoin in its entirety requires knowledge of some considerably technical and nuanced concepts because Bitcoin's protocol is a highly original combination of several independent technologies. Instead, we'll proceed another way: we will break down the problem and build up toward Bitcoin's particular solution, starting from a stripped-down, intentionally simple case, built upon what we learned in the previous chapter about blockchains.

Remember that a blockchain is a distributed public ledger? "Ledger" means that it's an immutable, or unchangeable, record of transactions between accounts. "Public" means that everyone with access can view the full record. "Distributed" means that it's not kept in a single place, but instead there are multiple people who have identical copies.

What is the simplest blockchain we could implement? The hypothetical problem becomes a lot easier if we can assume we know all the participants. Let's take an example of such a scenario.

Imagine a handful of companies that are located in the city of EverywhereTown. The companies operate in different industries. Each of them own some vans, but transportation is very much secondary to their primary businesses. Yet occasionally, any one of the companies might need access to a fleet of vans larger than what they own. Why not solve the problem by pooling their resources? The CEOs of the companies come together to create a van-sharing community, and shaking hands and popping the corks on a few bottles of champagne, the companies' CEOs jointly decide that they will use a blockchain as their technological solution. Let's call it the EverywhereVanChain. Note that they're not doing an ICO, so they don't need a more marketable name!

A team of software developers from the companies comes together to design the protocol. At minimum, the EverywhereVanChain ledger must keep track of the ownership of vans and loan reservations, and ensure that multiple reservations aren't accidentally registered for the same van for the same day. To keep things simple, the protocol designers have made the choice that vans are always lent for a full day. Another simplifying decision is that the only type of **asset** represented on the blockchain is a van. The developers can now agree on these basic operations that will be stored on the blockchain:

> ***Add van to pool***—a company has purchased or otherwise obtained a new van and makes it available to lend.
> ***Remove van from pool***—a van has been decommissioned or taken out of circulation for repairs or because of a sale.
> ***Reserve van for a day***—this creates a loan transaction.
> ***Cancel previous reservation***—a previous loan transaction has been cleared, freeing up the van.

The developers can now get to work on the software itself. Each active participant in a blockchain runs a piece of software called a **node**. In practice, this simply means software running on a server connected to the Internet. It could be hosted "on-premises" by a participant, or on a cloud provider, such as Amazon Web Services. The nodes all implement the same protocol, and each maintains a full copy of the ledger. The nodes are in constant communication over a network. The nature of the network itself is not fundamental: nodes could exchange data by carrier pigeons if there was nothing else available, but that would, of course, make it very slow to achieve consensus between nodes.

Since the number of companies joining the van-sharing community is small, they decide to use the simplest possible way to authenticate participants on the blockchain: **pre-shared keys**. Each company generates its own cryptographic private key that they can use to sign operations on the blockchain. The private key has a counterpart called a public key, which is not secret, and so each company shares these with the others. Thus, we can say it's an agreed part of this protocol that each blockchain node already knows the cryptographic public keys for all the other participants. There will be a more thorough explanation of cryptography in a later section, so don't worry if you don't fully understand what private and public keys actually are and how they function.

When Company X adds a van to the pool, its node will produce a new data block containing that operation and sign it with Company X's private key. The node software sends out the new block to the other nodes. Each node looks at the new block and verifies whether its signature matches Company X's public key, which was shared as part of the protocol; if it does, it will be appended to the blockchain. Note that, on this simple blockchain, a block and a transaction are the same thing. On real-world blockchains like Bitcoin, there are multiple transactions within a block.

So far, this is all very simple. Adding vans is an especially easy case. It doesn't require sophisticated consensus because it's an uncontestable operation: nobody should object to having more vans available in the pool. However, reserving vans is a different story. What if two companies try to reserve the same van at the same time? How does the blockchain decide who actually gets the van? This is a variation of the famous **double-spending problem**. The blockchain must not contain two accounts "spending the same asset"—in this case, lending the same van for the same day.

Conflicts will arise because it takes time for information to spread out to all nodes of the blockchain. Imagine that Company Y and Company Z both want to borrow the new van that Company X previously offered to the pool. The software nodes owned by Y and Z will both send a new block containing the "reserve van" operation. Some of the participants on the blockchain will see Y's block first, others will see Z's block first, but all of them will eventually see that there's a conflict. How to decide?

At this point, the protocol needs a **consensus algorithm**. One of the simplest solutions would be a vote. All of the nodes call one another with the question: "Which block did you see first?" Once the responses come in, either Y or Z will have more votes. Each node will then discard the losing block. Consensus has been achieved, and the blockchain is intact; in other words, every node's copy looks the same. This "peer voting" algorithm is simple but has some downsides. For one, it has the same problem as the United States Senate: there needs to be a tie-breaking mechanism in case there's an even number of nodes and the vote is split equally down the middle. In the Senate, the Vice President gets to vote to break a tie. On the EverywhereVanChain, maybe the protocol could contain a rotating tie breaker account—first it's Company A, then Company B, etc.

Another, and more serious, limitation of this peer voting consensus algorithm is that it can be manipulated. If someone can gain control of more than 50 percent of the nodes, they can make sure the vote always ends in their favor. This kind of trickery could be undetectable by participants who are not aware of the conspiracy to take over the blockchain. Imagine that the devious chief executive of Company Q wants to make sure his van requests always go through. He bribes software developers at half of the other companies to modify the software running on their nodes so that, whenever a peer vote comes up where Company Q is involved, the software will vote for Q regardless of which block it actually saw first. To the companies participating on the blockchain, everything would seem to be running as normal, but in reality, the protocol has been compromised. This is called a **majority attack**, or a 51 percent attack.

This brings us to a really important point: how can you really trust that the other nodes on your blockchain network are actually implementing the protocol correctly—in other words, doing the things they claim to be doing? You probably can't go to Company Q's offices and audit the software that's running in their data center. Any solution would need to be implemented through the blockchain itself.

There are ways to verify that nodes are not misrepresenting what they are doing, and this is one of Bitcoin's core innovations. In Bitcoin, not all nodes are actually allowed to update the blockchain. There are special nodes, called **miners**, that collect transactions into blocks and compete against each other for the right to add the next block to the chain. The winner of this competition is determined by having the miners perform highly repetitive computations: each of them tries to come up with a mathematical solution to a nonsense problem that was agreed upon as part of the protocol. In Bitcoin, the problem involves computing hashes, those digital fingerprint values discussed in the previous section, so you'll see the word "hashing" used in the context of mining. In other blockchain protocols the hard-to-compute problem can be something else entirely.

It is crucial that the problem presented to the miners is hard to solve, yet easy to verify by all the other nodes. Once a miner node comes up with a solution, the node's software will make a new block with all the transactions it has heard about, add its own "reward" transaction to the block, and send the block out to everybody else on the network. There are several more sophisticated aspects to this part of Bitcoin, including a consensus protocol that resolves situations where two miners claim the same block. If you want to know the exact technical details, we recommend an *Ars Technica* article from December 2017 called "Want to really understand how Bitcoin works?" [3]

As we mentioned in the previous section, Bitcoin is a Proof of Work blockchain. By comparison, the EverywhereVanChain is a Proof of Authority blockchain because the authorized accounts' keys were pre-shared between participants. This was acceptable only because it's a closed protocol for predetermined participants. In Bitcoin, transactions are validated by the miners, who spend energy on solving a predetermined math problem, trying to outrace each other for the prize of writing the next block. This approach is a major improvement over the naïve consensus we saw previously because it shifts the nature of the majority attack. It also neatly establishes a base of value for the singular type of asset represented on the Bitcoin blockchain: all Bitcoins are created through mining and paid as rewards to miners. Anyone can create a new account, but it starts with a zero balance. The only way to increase your balance is to either mine or receive a transaction of coins from someone else.

---

[3] https://arstechnica.com/tech-policy/2017/12/how-bitcoin-works The information is still valid and fairly approachable, as far as programmer-oriented content goes!

In EverywhereVanChain, we saw that the blockchain could be taken over if more than 50 percent of the nodes are compromised. This limitation is actually probably quite acceptable in the context of that hypothetical closed van-sharing community: it seems unlikely that companies in distinct fields would bother to secretly create a cartel just to tilt the van-sharing system in their favor. However, Bitcoin is different because it is open. One of its core features is that anyone can run a node and make an account; you don't need anyone's permission to join. In an open system like Bitcoin, the same limitation that seemed acceptable in EverywhereVanChain would spell instant doom to the blockchain's reliability. For example, someone with control of a "botnet," where thousands of PCs that have been hacked remotely to perform actions without their owners' knowledge, could command all those bot PCs to become Bitcoin nodes, and they would quickly outnumber legitimate actors.

Mining solves this problem. Instead of just the number of nodes, a majority attacker would now have to gain control of more than 50 percent of *active mining capacity*. Since mining is expensive but also automatically rewarded with Bitcoins, there's little incentive for miners to team up and plot to undermine the protocol's reliability—that would effectively turn their hard-acquired Bitcoins into nothing more than numbers on a hard disk. However, the miners might want to team up to *change* the protocol. Together they control a fundamental part of the blockchain's value, and they might want to effectuate a change by "voting with their feet"—that is, moving their mining power over to a different version of the software. A change which keeps the blockchain data but changes the protocol going forward is called a **fork**. Bitcoin Cash is a recent high-profile example of a fork that has support from miners.

Let's take a closer look at the notion of assets represented on a blockchain. Our hypothetical EverywhereVanChain and the grand old Bitcoin both share an important property: there is a single type of asset. On EverywhereVanChain, the target asset is a van, voluntarily submitted to the pool by participating companies. On Bitcoin, it's the eponymous coin, created by mining as described above.

A blockchain protocol could just as well represent multiple types of assets, and in fact, many blockchains do, as that is one of the most obvious points of differentiation from Bitcoin. How about we add a new asset type to the EverywhereVanChain? Let's make it a **token**.

Everyone has probably encountered physical tokens that are used instead of cash at various businesses—casino chips are the most obvious example. A token on a blockchain serves a similar purpose. Just like a casino chip only has value within a certain framework agreed upon by participants, a token's value is entirely up to definition. Note that the same applies to actual currency: a Canadian dollar coin is useful legal tender, but good luck paying with it at a New York deli. Not all blockchain assets must be tokens, as we've already seen: the vans on EverywhereVanChain are not tokens because the vans can't be transferred or exchanged with other participants. Yet the possibility of trading with other partners is fundamental to many blockchain use cases, so in practice assets often tend to be tokens.

What kind of token could we introduce to EverywhereVanChain? We don't really want to introduce any extra bureaucracy to the simple transaction of lending vans. Instead, the new token could be a positive, playful reward system—a friendly way to recognize those companies that have been active in sharing their vans. Let's call it the VansterPoint, and agree that the company who has collected the most VansterPoints during each year gets to take home a shiny trophy that can be proudly displayed at their holiday party.

In the real world, reward systems are already forming major token-like economies. Think of air miles, shopping loyalty points, credit card points, etc. However, the corporations that own these systems have rigid controls on the ways that members can use and trade these acquired tokens. There could be interesting opportunities in this space.

To add the VansterPoint token into the protocol, the developers will modify the EverywhereVanChain protocol code and upgrade all the nodes. In the new protocol, any account will automatically receive a VansterPoint when one of their vans is loaned. VansterPoints can also be spent by sending them to other accounts. This may not seem immediately useful, but it has effectively created a minimally useful currency that could be used in other playful interactions between the companies. For example, how about an inter-company softball match where the loser must pay 50 VansterPoints to the winning company? Wouldn't that sting to lose! *You must understand, there's not a lot of excitement in EverywhereTown.*

In this way, we have taken what was a small business efficiency problem shared by companies in the same town—vans sitting unused—and turned it into a mini-economy that can foster increased collaboration, and increasingly competitive softball matches, among the people at these companies. The blockchain is the technological ingredient that enabled a sense of fairness in the creation of this economy while also allowing the expansion and creation of new rules and capabilities over time.

This example scenario was intended to show a simple kind of blockchain use case defined in real-world terms. In the next sections, we'll look in more detail at various aspects of the underlying technologies, and then proceed to examine more practical uses of tokens in present-day blockchain applications.

# 3.

# What's Crypto?
# The Mathematical Breakthrough that Enabled Digital Privacy and Identification

Cryptography in itself isn't a present-day invention. In Chapter 1, we mentioned that the London-to-New York money order scenario set in 1750 could have made use of cryptography in the form of a shared code book between the parties. The initial concept can be predated to more than just a few hundred years, however. The need to share secret messages, and reliably identify parties you may not have met before, has been present in human societies as long as there have been discordant interests. In other words: for as long as there has been information to steal, plans to foil, and organizations for spies to infiltrate.

Julius Caesar already used a primitive encryption technique which is still today known as "Caesar's cipher." In the subsequent two millennia, mathematicians invented a plethora of more complex methods of encryption, but the fundamental principle did not change much from the days of noble Julius: when you received a coded message, you couldn't read it unless you knew the key that was used to encrypt it. Think of old-fashioned spy movies: they have a single code book used for both receiving and transmitting.

A revolution happened in the 1970s with a breakthrough called **asymmetric encryption**. In this method, there are two kinds of keys: private and public. In either case, the keys are simply very large numbers (on the order of trillion times trillion, at least). For user convenience, the private key is usually represented not as one giant number but in a shorter textual form: a mix of letters and digits, or a sequence of words.

There are two ways to use asymmetric encryption. The first is when the public key is used as "write-only" for sending information. Someone who has your public key can use it to encode a message, and only you, or another person who holds your private key, will be able to decode that message. This would be useful for Julius Caesar's campaign: he could distribute his public key far and wide without worrying about the secret being exposed.

It's also possible to flip the roles and use a public key that is "read-only." The holder of the private key will send an encoded message, and it can be decrypted by anyone who holds the public key. This development enabled **digital signatures**. Typically you would produce a message that states something on your behalf, such as: "I, Julius Caesar, have conquered Gaul on this day, the third of October!" and encrypt it with your private key. The message is now cryptographically signed. The recipient, in this example perhaps the Senate of Rome, would decode it using your public key, and they can trust that it was actually sent by you rather than an impostor. (Of course, asymmetric encryption was invented 2,000 years after Caesar's death, so he didn't actually do this, but you can.)

This is called **cryptographic proof**, and it's the foundational building block of all blockchains. Participants are identified by their cryptographic identities, which consist of a private key and a public key. Messages on the blockchain— transactions of whatever nature the protocol allows—are digitally signed, and their sender can thus be verified. This enables accountability directly between participants without the need for a supervising third party.

However, it also creates tremendous incentives for hacking because an exposed private key gives anyone access to the blockchain account. That one crucial number is all someone needs to execute transactions in your name. If they have your private key, they can connect to the blockchain from anywhere in the world and impersonate you. There is no third-party overseeing transactions, and therefore, no customer service number to call to restore your account balance after it has been emptied. The gods of cryptography are cruel, soulless mathematical entities, and they only care about whether rules are followed precisely. Small mistakes can be costly—a point we'll encounter again shortly in the context of smart contracts.

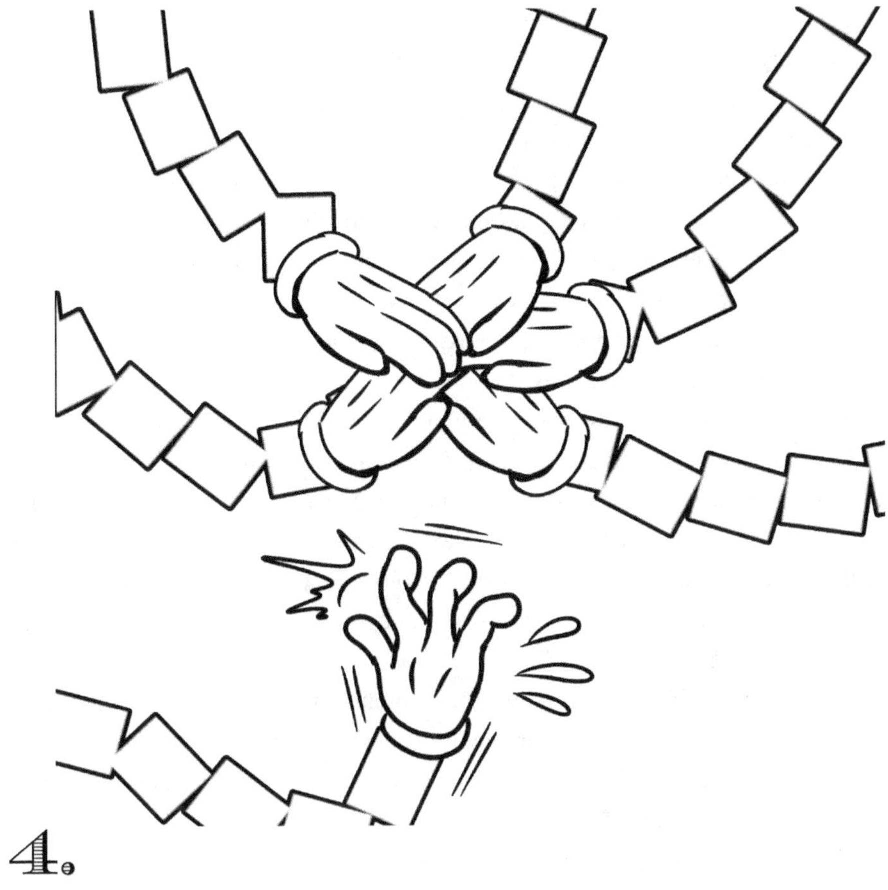

# 4.

# How the Blockchain Protects Information

We've already discussed the essential aspects of blockchains' purpose and design in previous chapters, so many concepts in this section are a recap of the various design principles that make the blockchain a reliable store of information.

Traditional computer systems suffer from the risk of a single point of failure. If information is stored on just one system, it is easily lost. The typical approach to mitigate these risks is replication—data is copied to multiple systems. The simplest replication setup would be a live backup: if the primary fails, you switch over to the secondary, then hope that the primary can be fixed quickly so that the secondary doesn't have time to fail while it's running without a backup of its own.

In modern Internet-based systems, replication designs are much more advanced and usually intimately tied to strategies of dividing data so that actively needed data is located on systems that can quickly make it available to its users. Think of all the data you might have stored on Facebook. If you live in, say, North America, it's probably unlikely that someone in Thailand will log in today and decide to access your photos from three years ago. Therefore, those images are probably not replicated in Facebook's southeast Asia data centers. If it happens that someone does want to see them in Bangkok, Facebook's system will fetch your data from the American data center, making the experience slower for the Thai user.

Blockchains are not like this. Nobody gets to decide which nodes should have which piece of the ledger. Instead, everybody keeps a full copy of the whole thing! This is the public, distributed aspect of the ledger. It's fundamental because it allows any node of the network to act as the "seed" for any new node that wants to join, and conversely, it means any node can go away without risking the integrity of the ledger. One term used to describe this kind of decentralized network is "peer-to-peer," but note that not all peer-to-peer networks are automatically replicated like blockchains are.

If this sounds like a potentially huge amount of data—well, you're absolutely right. The blockchain is a fundamentally inefficient way to store information. If Facebook were a blockchain application, someone in Thailand would have copies of your vacation photos from 2014, and conversely, you'd be forever keeping copies of theirs. Clearly this level of obsessive data replication is only necessary and useful for *some* types of information.

The data stored on the blockchain is protected by cryptography, and specifically by digital signatures as discussed in Chapter 3. In most cases, people's accounts on the blockchain are really just public keys. Bitcoin calls these **addresses**, which is perhaps more descriptive than **account**; unlike, say, your Facebook account, there's no kind of profile associated with a Bitcoin address, so it's really more like an anonymous mailbox. There is no cost for creating new addresses. You can generate a new private key at any time, thus also creating a new public key, and therefore a new address. Most blockchains are like this, but not necessarily all, as we saw in the intentionally limited design example of Chapter 2 where accounts were pre-created as part of the protocol itself.

To prevent tampering of the ledger after the fact, all data blocks stored on the blockchain contain a marker that identifies where the block belongs in the sequence. This identifying marker is the digital fingerprint of the preceding block. By tracing the markers back to the start of the chain, you can verify that the blockchain is intact and unmodified.

Unless the blockchain is private and participants are trusted, it's still not enough protection that data is replicated, digital signatures are used, and blocks form a verified sequence. To protect against fraudulent or conflicting transactions, the blockchain protocol also needs to be able to achieve consensus. The specific requirements to determine that consensus has been reached will depend on the protocol's intended purpose. There's no universally correct definition for what kind of transaction constitutes a "double spend" that needs to be prevented—imagine a token with infinite supply and therefore infinite spending, so a protocol wouldn't need to keep track of how many of those tokens are spent. Similarly, there's no universally correct answer to say which nodes should have authority over others. Bitcoin offered a robust answer to these questions with mining, where miner nodes compete for a coin prize and in the process provide the blockchain with verified transactions. Mining is providing consensus by Proof of Work, but comes with the downside that the work being performed is fundamentally useless. Other consensus algorithms exist that attempt to provide similar benefits without the waste of energy, but they come with their own tradeoffs, as we'll see later.

# 5.

# Smart Contracts and the Economic Structures They Enable

The blockchain protocols that we've seen so far have been fairly limited in their eventual scope of applications. Bitcoin's mining system for generating new blockchain assets is impressively clever, but once you have coins, there's really nothing you can *do* with them other than keep them for yourself or send them to someone else. Bitcoin is almost a paradox: coins are an asset of plain entropy, a permanent digital memento of a transient mathematical effigy. There is an interesting crystalline beauty to this paradoxical nature of coins created through Proof of Work, even though many disagree on whether it's ultimately the most useful approach.

The simplistic van-sharing blockchain design we examined in Chapter 2 is, in many ways, the opposite. No philosophical questions there—just a distributed ledger for a real-world asset. This example blockchain's usefulness is fundamentally limited by its protocol design, as all the operations you can perform on the vans and reward tokens are explicitly specified in the protocol code itself. There is no way a user who runs a node on this blockchain could get creative and invent some kind of new application on the same ledger. In that example scenario, such a limitation doesn't matter because the handful of companies that created the protocol also operate all the nodes. If they wanted to do something new on the ledger, they would just update their code, as they did when the "reward" token was added. Large public blockchains are not like this. Adding features to Bitcoin at this point is nearly impossible because you'd have to convince an enormous number of miners to join your new protocol.

What if the protocol itself was flexible enough to allow new applications to be built on top of it? This question arose soon after Bitcoin had gained some traction and was explored by subsequent blockchain protocols like NXT and Ethereum.

At the core of this flexibility is the concept of smart contracts, which is a contract-like set of promises encoded digitally, where (crucially!) the smart contract itself can also perform on those promises over time. Think of an insurance contract: "If it rains on Super Bowl Sunday, Ticketing Company X agrees to pay its customers $1 million." If this were encoded as a smart contract, Company X would theoretically have no wiggle room: the smart contract would execute on Super Bowl Sunday, check the weather, and transfer the money to its customers if required.

The concept was introduced by computer scientist Nick Szabo over 20 years ago in his seminal paper "Smart Contracts: Building Blocks for Digital Free Markets." As the title suggests, he was specifically thinking of economic contracts: electronic commerce, verified transactions between businesses, collaborative agreements, and so on. Smart contracts actually predate Bitcoin-style blockchains. The two are independent; blockchains are simply the most widespread implementation layer for smart contracts today. You don't need a distributed ledger to store and execute smart contracts, but the global nature of Bitcoin-style blockchains happens to be a useful lever that makes smart contracts much more powerful. Effectively, the blockchain's consensus power and financial incentives become the "enforcer" that smart contracts need, and that has made them useful in a way that wouldn't have been possible before.

To better understand what a smart contract could be, let's move from theory to existing practice to examine the most popular kind of smart contract currently being used—the **Initial Coin Offering** or ICO. Another name for essentially the same thing is "token-generation event." To distance this theoretical discussion from any associations one may have with the term "ICO," we'll only refer to token-generating smart contracts in this section.

What does it mean to generate a token? For a familiar comparison, let's refer back to the VansterPoint token introduced in Chapter 2. When this token was added to the protocol, the participating companies modified the actual blockchain code so that all accounts in the system now had a VansterPoint balance. This balance started out at zero and could accumulate more tokens over time, as rewards. This was the token-generation event, but in this case, no tokens were distributed immediately; rather, a feature was integrated into the blockchain protocol itself so that users could collect these tokens through their lending actions. Here we saw a token with no initial offering but perpetual **minting**; that is, the creation of new tokens.

A lot of tokens being created on blockchains today are the opposite: they have an initial offering but no minting. The supply of the token is defined when it is generated, and there will never be any more. This creates a limited supply, which can feel attractive to speculators. If the token becomes valuable, those who get in early will be guaranteed that their holdings are not diluted by inflation.

If the tokens are created all at once, who gets them? Assuming there is some immediate value to the tokens, the inventor of the token could just keep them all and sell them over time. But more often, the token is actually a precursor to some kind of protocol or application that is not yet finished, and the expectation is that the token will become more valuable as the development work is completed. In this case, the initial distribution of the tokens becomes similar to a fundraising event, in other words, seeking investments for an uncertain venture. The inventor of the token makes a limited time offer in which they will accept money in exchange for the newly generated tokens.

Smart contracts are a way to encode this kind of offer on a blockchain. Let's take an outlandish example. Imagine that the Acme AntiGravity Research & Holding (AAGRH) Foundation is close to a breakthrough that would enable levitation devices. The scientists have determined that they could initially build capacity to lift one million kilograms. To fund the work, they will sell one million LevitationTokens. Once AAGRH Foundation's device is ready, owners of

LevitationTokens will be able to digitally upload them into their levitation gadgets, and each token will contribute 1 kg of lift capability. Pretty awesome, right? One can imagine that the value of this token will go up when AAGRH Foundation finally releases their gadget and shows the skeptics of the world that levitation is possible.

AAGRH's bean counters have concluded that they need to raise one million Bitcoin to actually complete the device. Therefore, they'll be selling LevitationTokens for the price of 1 BTC each—not cheap, but hey, it's antigravity. It's important to note that AAGRH needs to sell all one million LevitationTokens, or they won't have enough money to actually build the device. Therefore, AAGRH Foundation uses a smart contract to encode this promise: if we receive one million BTC in orders, the LevitationToken will be generated, and everyone who sent a Bitcoin will receive a LevitationToken in their accounts. But, if we don't get enough orders within one month, everyone's money will be automatically returned, and the dream of antigravity will have to wait.

Here we see a smart contract that is encoding a contractual concept familiar from the real world: an **escrow**. People will send in their Bitcoins, and the AAGRH smart contract holds all the funds until one of two conditions is reached: either the full one million BTC is received or one month has passed. This smart contract has a **binary outcome**—if the crowdfunding succeeds, the new token is generated; otherwise, all the money is returned. Because the smart contract is a computer program, people who sent in their Bitcoins have a level of assurance that AAGRH Foundation won't be able to play any funny games with the money, and they'll receive either a LevitationToken or their money back.

This is all fine and good for AAGRH, but it raises some practical questions: how can this smart contract be implemented so that people can trust its execution, and how can the new LevitationTokens be distributed? The AAGRH Foundation could simply come up with a new blockchain to implement these features, but then they'd have to get people on board, running their own nodes and so on. This would be a major distraction from AAGRH's focus on antigravity development, and it would take a high level of dedication from AAGRH's potential investors to be running a completely custom blockchain for this purpose.

Wouldn't it be nice to have a blockchain platform that would provide the infrastructure for something like AAGRH's smart contract and token? That's what young cryptocurrency programmer Vitalik Buterin thought back in 2013. He introduced a research concept for a blockchain that can store and execute arbitrary smart contracts and token values. In 2015, the system went live under the name **Ethereum**. Today, its native token, called **ether (ETH)**, is the second most valuable cryptocurrency after Bitcoin.

Ethereum is often called a **distributed computing platform**, or even a global operating system—a term rather too vague to be useful. The smart contracts that can be defined on Ethereum are, in fact, full-fledged computer programs. They can fetch and store data within the blockchain and execute arbitrary operations. There is no fundamental limit to what you can run on the Ethereum platform, and much of its focus is on enabling so-called **dApps** (distributed apps), which would run on the blockchain and be accessible anywhere in the world.

The reality of Ethereum is somewhat removed from this promise. A globally replicated blockchain is fundamentally an expensive way to store information. Any program that needs to run on the blockchain needs to be executed on all the nodes. Executing smart contracts on Ethereum costs real money in the form of ETH, and following the 2017 price explosion in cryptocurrencies, it's become quite expensive to run any kind of dApp on Ethereum.

As it stands, the usefulness of Ethereum smart contracts today is not in dApps but rather in encoding more mundane business transactions like the "escrow + conditional token generation" example we saw described above. Thanks to the recognized trading value of ETH and its high liquidity, Ethereum works well for this kind of money transfer application built on smart contracts.

If you're designing a protocol and planning a token-generation event for it, you should consider carefully whether Ethereum makes sense as the actual implementation platform, or whether you'd simply want to raise money on Ethereum using smart contracts. The latter doesn't obligate you to use Ethereum for the actual protocol, but if you don't intend to use Ethereum for the implementation, you need to communicate this very clearly to people who might send funds to join your token-generation event. The Kin token created by the Kik messaging app company is an example of a project that raised significant funds on Ethereum in 2017, then switched to a different implementation platform in 2018 once they discovered that Ethereum can't support their projected usage volumes with low enough transaction fees. It's possible to do this, but much less of a headache if you plan ahead and inform your token holders in advance of the contingency that their tokens may need to be migrated.

# 6.

# Decentralization: The Core Principle

Previous sections have shown examples of both open and closed blockchains. The van-sharing blockchain designed in Chapter 2 was an extreme example of closed blockchains because the permitted participants were fixed in advance, or in programmer jargon, **hardcoded** into the protocol itself. Bitcoin and most other blockchains lie at the other end of the spectrum because anyone can run a node without needing to provide real-world authentication and without being vetted by existing participants.

There is an important secondary dimension to openness, however. A protocol can be open to new participants, yet contain an element of central control. Such a protocol would be called **centralized**. Bitcoin again serves as a good example of the opposite kind of design: we know Bitcoin is fully decentralized because there are no nodes on the network that would be "more equal than others," for example, by having the right to override decisions made by other nodes or by holding some kind of special powers to validate transactions more rapidly.

An example of a **de facto centralized blockchain** is Ripple. The blockchain protocol is designed and controlled by Ripple Labs Inc., an American corporation. The company markets their protocol to banks and other financial institutions as a solution for settling global financial transactions. To provide the kind of traditional security promise that banks require, Ripple's protocol uses a network of trusted validators who have special authority to validate transactions. The protocol has a native cryptocurrency, the ripple (XRP), but the Ripple corporation owns 60 percent of these tokens. These two factors—trusted validators, massively consolidated holding of tokens—put to doubt any claim of decentralization. Even if the protocol is useful and is eventually adopted by banks, it's not clear that XRP should gain in value; because transactions between banks will still take place in traditional fiat currencies, like the USD and EUR, there is no obvious reason for these participants to be holding XRP other than for the short duration of a transfer and paying the minimal fees required by the Ripple network. All this makes the high valuation of XRP seem more like a public relations vehicle for Ripple Labs Inc. rather than an indication of the actual usefulness of the protocol. A centralized blockchain is, by definition, easily manipulated by its controlling entity; however, in the case of Ripple, it's important to note that a high degree of centralized control is the very reason that makes the solution appealing to traditional financial institutions.

The example of Ripple shows that, although it seems obvious that decentralization is desirable, it is actually one of the most significant points of design divergence and contention in new blockchain protocols. Everyone wants to say that their blockchain is decentralized, and yet we see a lot of new designs offered that actually contain elements of centralization. It tends to make things easier. Having special "superpowered" nodes on the network makes it easier to reach consensus, and it can reduce or eliminate the need for mining. A fast and ecologically friendly blockchain sounds great, except for the nagging problem that introducing centralization in the form of "supernodes," federations of nodes, or any other guise destroys the promise of an impartial decentralized network.

To better understand this issue, let's examine IOTA, a real-world blockchain protocol that had a successful ICO and remains very popular on discussion forums among cryptocurrency enthusiasts, yet depends on centralization to a notably high degree. The IOTA project's focus is on **Internet of Things (IoT)** applications, i.e. very low-power devices. It uses a highly speculative technical solution: the team claims that their cryptography implementation using **ternary**, or three-value, logic—rather than traditional binary logic used by all computer chips manufactured to date—will be uniquely well-suited for IoT devices. Designing and building a new kind of computer processor is a very tall order, and so a discussion of the merits of this part of IOTA's approach is far beyond this book's scope. We'll only look at the specific question of centralization.

The core question in IOTA's design is how to balance the extremely low-power needs of IoT applications with the power-hungry approach of using Proof of Work (PoW) to validate transactions. The approach chosen by IOTA relies on tiny PoW hashing tasks. An attacker who wanted to create fake transactions would need to control no more than 33.3 percent of the hashing power on the network—a disturbingly low number considering that there are no separate "heavyweight" mining nodes—so the total hashing power at any given time is intended to be small. To account for this risk, the protocol currently contains a centralized **Coordinator,** which decides that some transactions are more important than others:

> [A] milestone is a special transaction issued by a special node called Coordinator. The Coordinator is run by Iota Foundation, its main purpose is to protect the network until it grows strong enough to sustain against a large scale attack from those who own GPUs [Graphics Processing Unit, dedicated hardware for specialized tasks that can be graphics or something with a similar computational profile]. Milestones set general direction for the tangle growth and do some kind of checkpointing. Transactions (in)directly referenced by milestones are considered as confirmed. [4]

The IOTA Foundation claims that this central, single point of validation that they operate will eventually go away, but there's no clear roadmap for how this would

---

[4]  IOTA developer Slack channel, Sep 2016; https://github.com/iotaledger/wallet/issues /8#issuecomment-247619535

happen. The Coordinator is not open source, so third parties can't verify what it does either. Given the team's grand claims of IoT-enabled fridges and heaters eventually globally collaborating on verifying payments using the IOTA system, it's suspicious that its first implementation is entirely controlled by the Foundation itself. This doesn't automatically mean that the design is invalid, but it's a telltale sign of a blockchain project where vision and reality are still far from converging, which is something for investors to be aware of and is also something that ICO founders need to make a special effort to communicate.

# 7

# A Token Economy in the Wild

Previous sections have already covered various existing and hypothetical tokens as seen through specific lenses, like the use of smart contracts and degree of centralization. In this section, we'll take more of a "bird's eye," full-economy look at a successful and widely recognized protocol that was launched via an ICO, and how it intends to provide value for participants and token holders.

### *Basic Attention Token (BAT) by Brave*

BAT is an Ethereum-based token created by Brave Software, an American company that develops a free web browser. The Brave browser is based on the same open source code as Google's Chrome, but contains a built-in ad blocker and is designed to share less data with advertisement networks than regular browsers.

The browser is addressing a genuine problem: ads are a major source of irritation to users, and online privacy is deteriorating due to uncontrolled data collection through ad networks. Of course, the reason why publishers place ads on their sites seemingly in spite of what their users want is that they need the revenue. Monetizing online content through any other means is difficult. Brave tries to solve this problem by giving the user more agency while also splitting ad revenue between the publisher and the user using the Basic Attention Token (BAT). It is described by Brave as a "unit of exchange between publishers, advertisers and users [whose] utility is derived from—or denominated by—user attention."

In practice, the Brave browser anonymously monitors user attention, then sends BAT tokens as rewards to both the user for viewing the content and the publisher for providing it. For advertisers, Brave promises to deliver higher-quality data about user engagement than is possible with traditional web ads. The main focus of the BAT token economy is on enabling sustainable business models for online publishers. Most of the ad money that flows from advertisers in the form of BAT tokens is sent to publishers, and publishers can also create premium content experiences using the BAT payment system so that users can spend their BATs on the same site from which they received them.

BAT has several virtues that make it a good example of a well-designed token: it is easy to understand how the various participants in this economy benefit, and the technology is shipping in the Brave browser so it's not just "vaporware" or "whitepaper fantasy," like some ICOs. The fundamental challenge is acquiring the user base. Getting people to switch browsers is simply very difficult! Google spends enormously on marketing Chrome and also has the unique advantage of being able to place free ads on the Google.com homepage. Even with all that marketing muscle, Google hasn't been able to displace Firefox, Safari, and Microsoft Edge. Brave faces a tremendous uphill challenge against these entrenched competitors. Brave's credibility in this endeavor is entirely based on the team's track record. The company was founded by Brendan Eich, the inventor of the JavaScript programming language and a founder of Mozilla and Firefox. Few people in the world can claim to understand browsers better than Mr. Eich.

With an easy-to-understand token economy, working technology, and a world-class team, it's no surprise that BAT's June 2017 launch became one of the highest-profile ICOs of the year. Brave raised the equivalent of $35 million USD on Ethereum within 30 seconds.

For token holders who didn't get to buy the token at a special favorable rate in the ICO, it has been less of a windfall. The BAT token is listed on several exchanges where it can be bought and sold against Bitcoin. The BAT/BTC exchange rate started at about 16,000 BAT in June, hit a low point of 100,000 BAT in December 2017, and two years later had recovered to around 50,000 BAT/BTC, or 0.0002 BTC/BAT. Although not as catastrophic a loss of value as seen by many other "altcoins," it's clear that investors would have been better off holding Bitcoin. This demonstrates one of the great challenges when designing cryptocurrency token economies: how to reward long-term token holders. BAT is a utility token with a clear and proven source of revenue from advertisers, but perhaps it lacks incentives for users and publishers to hold onto their BAT tokens rather than cash them out as soon as they can. Chapter 9 explores this conundrum in more depth.

# How Do Tokens Rise in Value?

The crazy days of 2017 and early 2018 certainly set a high bar with regard to expectations for future appreciation of cryptocurrency tokens. Given the great variety of projects that were introduced, and the undisputable lack of experience on the part of many new crypto-investors, it seems unlikely that all those hopes and dreams of meteoric increase in token market values would come true. The wheat will be separated from the chaff, eventually. This begs the question: why should we expect *any* tokens to rise in value? What mechanisms control the price of digital tokens traded on blockchains?

If a blockchain is simply used as a technological solution to a social problem, the question becomes moot. We saw an example of such a blockchain protocol in Chapter 2. The EverywhereVanChain solved the practical problem of van-sharing for the participants, but there was no expectation of the assets described on the blockchain ever increasing in value, and therefore no provisions were made in the design for implementing exchanges so that outside investors could trade tokens.

For most real-world blockchains, there exists a speculative component to holding tokens. The presence of outside investors who buy and sell the crypto assets without participating in the utility aspect of the network is seen as beneficial, or at least as something that doesn't need to be actively discouraged. Consider the ICO and token described in the previous section: Brave's BAT. It has an obvious utility aspect, but it's equally obvious that the people who invested $35 million on Brave's BAT token launch day didn't put in that money because they want to get tokens that they can one day spend on banner advertising. Rather, the primary motivation for ICO participants is the expectation of token value appreciation as the blockchain-based networks become operational and hopefully explode in popularity.

In the previous discussion of BAT, we also noted that the token has, so far, fallen short of these expectations, having consistently underperformed relative to Bitcoin. This could be seen as a design flaw in the protocol; it doesn't provide enough incentive to hold the tokens rather than exchange them immediately for something more liquid (Bitcoin or fiat, i.e. traditional currency). If BAT were a traditional company's stock listed on an exchange like the Nasdaq, it would certainly be considered somewhat of a failure at this point.

BAT is not a stock, however, and judging it by the stock market's criteria would be misleading. This is because BAT is a **utility token**. Its value is not even tied to the financial performance of Brave Software, the company that issued these tokens, but rather the future performance of an entire ecosystem that hopefully will form around the use of BAT in digital advertisement.

Realistically, we just don't have enough historical data to predict how utility tokens will perform over longer timespans. There is one shining example of a utility token whose value has appreciated beyond wildest expectations in just a couple of years, and that is Ethereum's native token *ether* (ETH). However, that could be considered a perfect storm of exploding interest in blockchains and the freeform functionality in the Ethereum protocol, which enabled ETH to become the foundation of thousands of other ICOs. The same conditions don't exist for something like BAT, as its protocol is necessarily more limited in its potential scope of applications[5].

To compensate for the inherent uncertainty of investing in utility tokens whose utility doesn't yet fully exist, many ICOs have come up with various mechanisms that will effectively prop up the token's value over a period of time, typically the first year or two. These can include "hard" approaches, such as using smart contracts to create artificial deflationary events, like "burning" tokens after a given amount of time, or they can be more about "soft" public relations work, such as a roadmap that predicts the token's adoption by an exchange, which typically would increase the value of the token due to improved liquidity. We'll discuss these approaches in further detail in a later chapter.

In addition to utility tokens, there are also tokens whose value is tied to an asset outside the blockchain. These are called, obviously enough, **asset tokens** in the general case, but if the underlying asset is a regulated security, they can also be called security tokens to make this clear. With this kind of token, any appreciation in value is more obviously tied to the performance of the underlying asset. For example, imagine a token that gives you royalties based on the sales of a famous comic book artist's work. This is fundamentally no different from a traditional stock that pays dividends based on a company's profit, and therefore, such a token would be much easier to judge as an investment compared to a utility token.

There are cryptocurrency tokens whose value is directly tied to a backing asset so that there's essentially no room for speculative fluctuation in the price. One such token is Tether (USDT), a cryptocurrency that is used by some Bitcoin exchanges as an intermediate store of value when selling other cryptocurrencies. As its name and the USDT symbol imply, Tether is directly tethered to the United States dollar. The issuer of the Tether tokens is the eponymous Tether corporation, which promises that it has USD cash in the bank—some bank, somewhere in the world, but not saying exactly where—to match each and every Tether USDT token that has been created. With such a structure, the USDT token should hold its exchange value exactly at $1 USD.

During 2018 and 2019, the corporation that emits Tethers was gradually forced to admit that it doesn't actually hold enough cash in USD to back all the Tethers in

---

[5]  It is the humble opinion of these writers that Ethereum's unlimited scope of theoretical functionality has created overblown expectations of its actual suitability for applications, but that is neither here nor there.

circulation. Instead some percentage of Tethers are backed by crypto-based loans and other seemingly dubious assets. The story is still developing, but regardless of how it turns out, Tether is already an interesting case study in cryptographic asset tokens and the degree of trust required to participate in trade with such tokens. If USDT were a traditional financial instrument, it would probably be priced substantially below its nominal tethered value of $1 USD due to the liquidity risk of the issuing corporation. Yet in the world of cryptocurrency, the value of USDT has barely budged against a stream of scandalous revelations about Tether's behind-the-scenes management. Who is holding the risk? How does one do their due diligence in an asset like this? Decentralized assets can be more transparent than traditional ones, but they can also be intentionally designed to be more opaque.

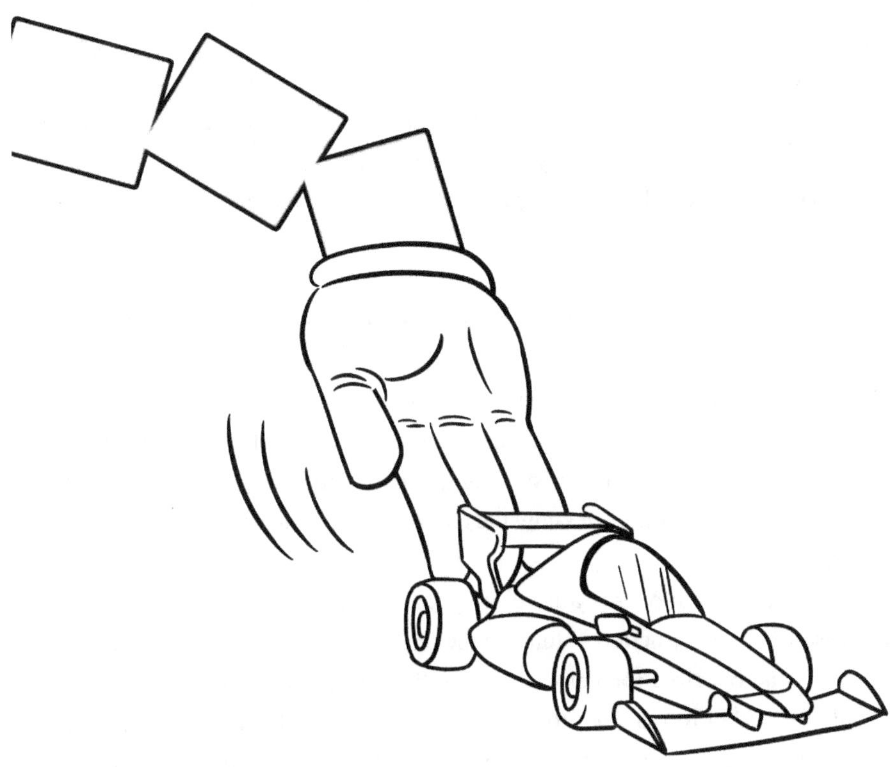

# 9.

# The Effects of "Token Velocity"
# What Makes a Good Utility Token?

TOKEN VELOCITY is a term that succinctly describes and gives a numeric value to a problem that is inherent in many utility tokens: *why should anyone hold it?*

We already alluded to this issue in the previous discussion of BAT, the Basic Attention Token created by Brave Software. The market performance of BAT so far suggests that there may not be enough incentives for users to hold on to the tokens that they receive from Brave. Instead, users are looking to cash in their tokens into something more liquid as soon as they can. This situation may correct itself if the Brave browser becomes more popular; strong word-of-mouth and growing adoption of the browser software would reinforce perception of the token by association, and make users feel like owning the tokens is like taking part in the success story of the software. Such an effect would be psychological, though. Psychology is, of course, a major component of any investment's success, but it is not quantifiable in the same way token velocity is.

Kyle Samani of Multicoin Capital derived a mathematical definition for token velocity as follows:

$$\textit{Velocity = Total Transaction Volume / Average Network Value}$$

Don't worry, there won't be any more equations in this chapter! Compared to a verbal explanation of the same concept, there is an advantage to having an algebraic definition, and it is this: using this equation, we can extract the value of any component assuming we know the two others, or at least can take a reasonable guess at them.

The three components are velocity, total transaction volume, and average network value. Transaction volume is the one that we can directly measure, and it provides the baseline for velocity. Velocity is actually a "sweet spot" value: it should be neither too low nor too high. We would expect velocity's exact value to evolve over time as the protocol's use grows, and it is the *change* in the protocol's velocity over time that provides a glimpse of the token's true value.

If an asset is so illiquid that no one buys or sells it, total transaction volume will be zero and hence token velocity will also be zero. This is obviously not desirable. On the other hand, if an asset is extremely liquid, but nobody holds it for very long, what happens in the token velocity equation is that the total transaction volume grows but the network value—that is, the value captured by the network—stays the same. This leads to an ever-growing velocity score, indicating a problem with the token's economic foundation because participants don't want to hold onto it.

When designing a token, we can use the token velocity equation as a rough measuring stick for estimating the network's future value. For example, assume that we've identified a market that could support $1 billion USD worth of transactions annually using our token. Yet, an estimate of the velocity suggests that users wouldn't be holding the token except for short transactions, placing the velocity somewhere around 1,000. Plugging these values into the token velocity equation gives us a back-of-the-napkin estimate: the proposed network's average value turns out to be only one million dollars even though it would be enabling transactions worth a billion. Suddenly it looks less interesting as an investment.

For most utility tokens, reducing velocity is a primary design concern. In his article[6] introducing this concept, Samani offers five ways that token velocity can be throttled down:

1. Introduce a profit-share (or buy-and-burn) mechanism;
2. Build staking functions into the protocol that lock up the asset;
3. Create balanced burn-and-mint mechanics;
4. Encourage holding through gamification;
5. Become a store of value.

The last one of these is not really a realistic option for new token designs. The *de facto* store of value in cryptocurrency is Bitcoin, and any new entrant would need tremendous adoption to see any velocity-reducing benefit from this effect. The other four mechanisms are available for consideration for any ICO, however.

---

[6]  https://multicoin.capital/2017/12/08/understanding-token-velocity/

# 10.

# When Decentralization Meets Real-World Laws

The ICO is a new kind of financial structure with a degree of configurability that, in many ways, goes beyond the traditional instruments defined in existing regulations. During 2016 and 2017, ICOs leaped, almost overnight, into the public eye with major success stories and a great variety of approaches to regulation, leaving lawmakers and financial regulators worldwide playing a game of catch-up.

Within the cryptocurrency community, there emerged two extreme viewpoints: some "ICO optimists" believed that blockchain-based fundraising and smart contract-based token distribution schemes are so different from traditional financial instruments that the old rules simply wouldn't apply, and that, by inference, new rules could be created "on the fly" by applying whatever laws seemed most suitable—or perhaps most convenient. This led to some dangerous legal mishaps, such as ICOs that didn't have any kind of legal structure in place to protect the project initiators and investors, or ICOs that pretended to be collecting "donations" when they were clearly selling tokens.

The other extreme viewpoint was the "ICO pessimists." In this view, ICOs are fundamentally unnecessary, and the ones that were executed would be inevitably subject to crackdown by government authorities as illegal securities. This type of categorical pessimism can be found among traditional investors, but it also seems to be particularly prevalent in a certain hardcore group of Bitcoin investors—sometimes called "Bitcoin maximalists"—who believe that Bitcoin is the only cryptocurrency of value and that other blockchain-based coins and tokens are basically poor imitations of the original Bitcoin.

A consensus is now emerging, and it falls somewhere in the middle of the two extremes. Various government actors are presenting initial recommendations regarding ICOs and tokens, and thus the rules are starting to solidify in various jurisdictions. The situation is still in flux, but it has greatly improved since 2017 because there are now official statements and guidelines available that entrepreneurs can use to design ICOs that will meet regulatory approval.

One of the most influential rule-makers in global finance is the U.S. Securities and Exchange Commission, or SEC. To better understand the SEC's role, let's take a short trip back in history.

In the 1920s, the legendary American Wild West had calmed down. Instead of prairies and frontier towns, a new kind of Wild West was enjoying its heyday on Wall Street and in the offices of shady brokers around the country. The stock market was booming, but there were practically no limitations on solicitations made to the public. Silver-tongued salesmen went around selling golden investment opportunities to moms and pops eager to get in on the boom. It all came crashing down in the stock market collapse of 1929, and America fell into the Great Depression.

The SEC was created in the aftermath of that painful episode. The Securities Act of 1933 made it illegal to offer to sell securities to the public without SEC oversight and approval. That law created the state of affairs that still exists today: you cannot sell shares or other securities to Americans unless you've registered for a public offering with the SEC or the sale meets the requirements for an exception under the 1933 law. One of these exceptions is that purchasers must be verified as "accredited investors"—in practice, people with a net worth of at least $1 million, excluding the value of their primary home.

To greatly simplify the issue: if you're selling anything that looks like a security in America, you must either ensure that your customers/investors are verified millionaires or go through an onerous process to register the security offering with the SEC.

What exactly is a security then? There's the rub for ICOs. In 2016 and 2017, many took a highly optimistic view about whether blockchain tokens would be considered securities by the American regulator. The SEC did not respond immediately but started offering increasingly strong hints of its position during 2017.

The best-understood criterion for whether something is a security in the SEC's eyes is known as the "Howey test," named after a landmark 1946 lawsuit *SEC v. Howey Co.* The U.S. Supreme Court formulated the test as follows:

*A transaction is an investment contract if:*

- *It is an investment of money;*
- *There is an expectation of profits from the investment;*
- *The investment of money is in a common enterprise;*
- *Any profit comes from the efforts of a promoter or third party.*

FindLaw expands on the definition with this note:

> Although the Howey Test uses the term "money," later cases have expanded this to include investments of assets other than money. The term "common enterprise" isn't precisely defined, and courts have used different interpretations. Most federal courts define a common enterprise as one that is horizontal, meaning that investors pool their money or assets together to invest in a project. However, other courts use different definitions.[7]

The last point of the Howey test means that the profit potential is out of the investor's hands. In other words, if the transaction is such that profit is only possible if the buyer actively puts in work, it is probably not a security.

---

[7]  http://consumer.findlaw.com/securities-law/what-is-the-howey-test.html

In February 2018, the SEC came down hard in favor of the strictest interpretation of the Howey test as applied to blockchain tokens. The SEC has issued subpoenas to several companies and individuals who raised capital through an ICO. For now, it appears that the SEC is not interested in debating the difference between utility tokens and asset tokens; anyone who raised money from U.S. investors with a utility token can be caught in SEC's crosshairs. This is starkly different when compared to other jurisdictions like Gibraltar, Switzerland, and Singapore, where regulators have offered explicit guidelines on how they treat different types of blockchain tokens.

The SEC's actions will have major ramifications in the American crypto community. Future token offerings must make sure to follow SEC rules, including the accredited investor rule. Anyone who already issued utility tokens in America would do well to contact their lawyer and figure out if they need to redo the offering under SEC rules while refunding previous investors. Howard Marks of StartEngine has written a post with a clear explanation of this process[8].

**Remember that nothing in this book can be considered legal advice. You should always consult a lawyer if you are an American citizen or resident and have questions about SEC regulations, or if you are a non-American and you intend to operate in the U.S. in any way. Please don't take chances in the most litigious market in the world.**

For foreign companies issuing tokens, the most obvious way to deal with the situation is to exclude Americans altogether from participating in the ICO. Many ICOs had already started doing this in 2017. The softer option is to require documentation from Americans that they are accredited investors, but this obviously adds some extra paperwork to the "Know Your Customer" (KYC) step of an ICO.

Thus, even non-American crypto investors are increasingly finding themselves faced with questions related to SEC requirements. It is an important baseline for other governments around the world as they make decisions on which approach they want to take. Some Asian governments are issuing hard bans on ICOs and cryptocurrency trading; others are taking a more nuanced view and have started work to classify tokens, as exemplified by a document called "A Guide to Digital Token Offerings"[9] released by the Monetary Authority of Singapore (MAS) in November 2017.

---

[8]  https://hackernoon.com/the-sec-exposes-the-ico-rabbit-hole-51cfc3ff53d8
[9]  https://www.scribd.com/document/364476638/A-Guide-to-Digital-Token-Offerings-14-Nov-2017

In Europe, Switzerland has become an important "crypto hub" thanks to the presence of important blockchain platform drivers like the Ethereum Foundation, which is registered as a Swiss non-profit. Some EU member countries, such as Estonia and France, have indicated publicly that they hope to be crypto-friendly nations, but it remains to be seen how—or if—that eventually translates into legislation.

If you're looking to invest in an ICO, you should make sure that you understand in which jurisdiction the token sale is operating. Some ICO websites and whitepapers may not be forthcoming with this information. For example, you may see sites that claim a token sale is run by a foundation, but upon further inspection, there's no detail available whether such a foundation has actually been registered anywhere. Steer clear of any such ICO. If they haven't even done the basic homework of establishing a legal presence before collecting money, it means they're putting the cart before the horse, and their technology is probably equally poorly equipped.

# 11.

# Blockchain Technology Platforms Compared

We've already discussed two blockchains in detail, Bitcoin and Ethereum. These two are, by far, the most significant platforms today. Both have native cryptocurrencies that are easy to buy and sell thanks to "mass-market" exchanges like Coinbase, and hence Bitcoin (shortened either BTC or XBT) and Ether (ETH) are what the typical consumer is likely to buy if they decide to "put some money into crypto." In this chapter, we'll take a brief look at what separates these two major platforms and how they compare to two other well-known blockchain projects with different structures.

## *Bitcoin vs. Ethereum*

Bitcoin is the grandfather of them all, the canonical example of a cryptocurrency. You can find a detailed explanation of Bitcoin fundamentals in Chapters 2 to 4. If there's one thing that makes Bitcoin stand out as a blockchain protocol, it is the fact that it has a single-minded focus on a single application, namely storing and transferring values of its native coin to other participants on the network who are identified by their cryptographic public keys. Although some loopholes exist in the Bitcoin protocol that would allow for tiny amounts of other data to be stored on the blockchain, doing so is not widespread practice and would cost too much for most applications to use. Effectively, Bitcoin is a pure **store of value**. It has become the gold standard for other cryptocurrencies. Like gold, Bitcoin is perhaps expensive to move around compared to some other alternatives, but is universally accepted.

Ethereum is in many ways the opposite: if Bitcoin is "pared down to the bone" for the value-storage application, Ethereum is loaded with bells and whistles in the form of smart contracts that can theoretically execute any kind of computer code in a distributed and verified manner. The promise and implementation of smart contracts was discussed in Chapter 5.

Both Bitcoin and Ethereum have faced technical challenges as their popularity and fiat currency exchange rates (i.e., USD-to-coin) surged in 2017 and 2018. Due to its more limited scope, Bitcoin has been comparatively better equipped to face these challenges. The high transaction prices and high volatility of BTC-USD have meant that the original promise of using Bitcoin as an everyday currency has largely faded away, at least for the moment: it's just not very convenient to buy something in Bitcoin when you might end up paying $10 in transaction fees, and you won't know the exact Bitcoin price until the very last minute because vendors set their prices in fiat currency. For this reason, some large online vendors, like Steam, the world's most popular PC gaming platform, decided to stop accepting Bitcoin at the end of 2017. Still, it bears repeating that this is not a problem for what seems to be a majority of Bitcoin owners, who treat it more like an investment into a rare commodity than a currency—just like gold.

For Ethereum, the challenges appear more daunting simply because there's currently such a wide gap between the promises made by the Ethereum community and the platform's present ability to deliver. To a substantial degree, the price of ETH is predicated on the former: someone buying Ether is probably not viewing it purely as a store of value; rather they expect the Ethereum platform itself to become more valuable over time thanks to the applications that are (hopefully!) going to be built on top of it. The Ethereum community calls this ecosystem of Ethereum-based apps "Web 3.0," an appealing marketing term certainly; but the reality is currently so far from being a mass-market platform that it might as well not exist. There are no Ethereum-based "Web 3.0" apps in widespread use or really even accessible to laypersons.

There are several factors that contribute to this dearth of usable "Web 3.0" apps. For one, Ethereum is still young. These are the early days when developers and economic visionaries are still trying to figure out applications. Yet, Ethereum is already priced like a major mass-market success. The high price of ETH results in high transaction fees even for trivial operations on the blockchain, and, in a kind of vicious cycle of "too successful too soon," those high fees make it even harder to introduce the new kinds of apps that could take advantage of the platform's promise. There are also more fundamental issues: the design of Ethereum is already being stretched almost to a breaking point by the current volume of operations, which means that there are some difficult technology transitions ahead for the community.

For better and worse, the Ethereum platform is effectively still in "beta" and will remain so for years to come as the Ethereum Foundation and other contributors experiment with designs that could cope with the projected high transaction volume while still offering an affordable fee structure and maintaining the promise of a "global supercomputer." It's a difficult combination of requirements, and several possible fixes are in the works: since 2018, Ethereum developers have investigated a set of solutions, including "sharding," Proof-of-Stake, and something called **Plasma**, a network of sub-blockchains. In comparison, Bitcoin was basically at version 1.0 on the day it arrived. It sure helps to be simple and focused—and first to market too.

If Ethereum worked perfectly today and delivered on its grand promise of a unified platform for arbitrary smart contracts, it would cover a lot of use cases for blockchains. But since that's not the case, there is still ample room for other contestants to garner a foothold.

We'll next look at two of the more high-profile "alternative" blockchains, Stellar and EOSIO. These two are an interesting pair because they're very promising yet completely different in scope, ambition, and readiness.

## *Stellar*

Stellar is one of the most established blockchains currently in operation. It has corporate backing from Stripe, a popular online payment processing company. Stellar was founded in 2014 with technology derived from open source code from Ripple, a company whose private blockchain protocol targets financial institutions exclusively. Stellar's use case is less specific than Ripple's, but it's not a general-purpose computing platform like Ethereum.

Stellar's goal is to connect the world's payment systems and new kinds of assets. The platform has a native token named the lumen (XLM). Its primary purpose is not to be a store of value on its own but rather to facilitate conversions between asset types. Creating new tokens to represent assets is particularly easy with Stellar's custom smart contract definition language. This programming environment is fundamentally more limited than Ethereum, which means less room for unanticipated use cases, but it also has one enormous advantage: less opportunity for bugs that hackers can exploit to steal funds or disrupt contract execution.

Stellar also has a built-in distributed exchange. This is potentially huge for ICOs because it means token issuers can have instant liquidity for their tokens—assuming there are buyers and sellers, of course.

Compare this to Ethereum, where the platform contains no built-in system to trade between token types. Even though there's a standard called ERC20 for Ethereum tokens, it doesn't mean those tokens will be accepted by anyone. You can issue all the ERC20 standard tokens you want, but if nobody will go the extra mile and provide a service to exchange your tokens for some other representation of value such as Ether, the tokens are not genuinely liquid. This situation has put great power in the hands of third-party cryptocurrency exchanges because an ERC20 token has value only once it's listed by at least one or two exchanges. The exchanges know their value and typically require substantial listing fees from token issuers. If widely adopted, Stellar offers a decentralized solution to this hindrance where a handful of gatekeepers control which tokens can be purchased and sold.

Another point in Stellar's favor is high performance and low fees. Thousands of transactions can be processed for a lumen price that equates to only fractions of a USD cent. The average settlement time for transactions is measured in seconds rather than minutes, as with Ethereum.

If all this sounds too good to be true, remember that blockchain design is all about tradeoffs. One of the tradeoffs made by Stellar was already mentioned: its programming capabilities are simpler and more limited than Ethereum's, which largely explains why smart contract execution is so much faster. Another tradeoff that Stellar makes involves the degree of decentralization. There is no mining, which keeps fees down but also means that the network consensus must be achieved by some other means than by giving financial incentives to miners and letting them race to earn the next block, as Bitcoin and Ethereum do. Stellar's consensus algorithm is decentralized, but there is a degree of *de facto* centralization because the network's important validator nodes are mostly operated by Stellar Foundation or its partner corporations. It's true that anyone can run a node, but without the rewards of mining, you're effectively just donating server time to the Stellar Foundation by having your own validator node on the network.

How important is mining anyway? Proof-of-Work is a powerful economic hack that has propelled Bitcoin to its sky-high market cap, but for newer blockchain designs, the evolving consensus among cryptocurrency experts seems to be that we have to move beyond mining. Stellar doesn't have mining, and it reaps credible benefits from this design choice. Ethereum is looking to move to a Proof-of-Stake model in an upcoming network-wide upgrade. And similarly, EOSIO, an upcoming alternative blockchain we're going to discuss next, does not use mining either. Signs point to Proof-of-Work as an approach that will become Bitcoin's exclusive domain in the not-so-distant future.

## *EOSIO*

EOSIO deserves its place in this chapter because of its high technical ambition and the extraordinary amount of funds it raised in its long-running ICO.

The EOSIO blockchain protocol is developed and maintained by Block.one, a private company. It started a token offering in the summer of 2017 before the platform's technical design had been finalized, and over the next 12 months, Block.one raised the equivalent of $4.1 billion, mostly in Ethereum. The stated purpose of raising so much money was both developing the core platform as well as seeding the ecosystem. The native token of the new EOSIO blockchain is called the EOS.

In short, EOSIO aims to be a better, cheaper, faster Ethereum. It is a general-purpose execution environment for smart contracts, but the development environment is based on industry standards like the C++ programming language and the WebAssembly runtime environment rather than the "homegrown" approaches adopted by Ethereum.

The EOSIO blockchain is divided into subnetworks to enable high capacity and transaction volume. There are 21 **block producer** supernodes selected by a community voting process. These supernodes have a great responsibility in maintaining the network: they are effectively promising to process transactions in under half a second, no matter how high the volume gets. The EOSIO platform doesn't have mining and uses a model called **delegated Proof-of-Stake** (DPoS) instead. Running a block producer supernode is expensive: it is estimated to cost over $1 million USD yearly. The organizations that maintain these nodes get compensated in EOS tokens. It's a tradeoff: rather than having miner nodes racing each other doing redundant energy-expensive computational work as in Bitcoin and Ethereum, the elected supernodes have a guaranteed income from their transaction processing labor. The fee structure is like a tax on the entire ecosystem: everyone else's EOS tokens are diluted slightly to pay the supernodes. This is how EOSIO can make their claim to eliminate all fees for users: it's free in the same sense as universal healthcare is free in European countries.

After such a tremendous ICO raise during 2017-2018, expectations for EOSIO were running sky-high when it finally launched in June 2018. After some high-profile hiccups during the launch months when the software was still being finalized, the EOSIO network seems to be running roughly as advertised.

In 2020, there still remain widespread concerns about the project being too centralized, in particular because most of the 21 block producer supernodes are operated in China. This is seen as an Achilles' heel that could expose the entire EOSIO blockchain to intervention by the Chinese government. The block producers have also been criticized for not doing enough to promote the development of new dApps (distributed apps) that would take advantage of the EOSIO blockchain's technical capabilities. It seems that the most popular dApps on EOSIO are focused on gambling.[10]

---

[10] https://www.coindesk.com/everyones-worst-fears-about-eos-are-proving-true

# 12.

# A Critical Eye on Technology Claims: Examining Protocol Whitepapers

Someone has a new idea for a blockchain protocol. How do you evaluate whether it's any good? Practically everyone has something called a whitepaper on their website, which in theory is supposed to tell you everything you need to know, but deciphering these documents can feel overwhelming.

This chapter must start with an attempt to define the term **whitepaper**. Everyone in the cryptocurrency community calls their project pitches and design proposals whitepapers, and the term has become so intrinsic that today it seems unthinkable to propose a protocol or token without a whitepaper to back it up. Yet the actual format and structure of the whitepaper can seemingly be anything: from a dry, math-heavy computer science text to a glitzy PowerPoint presentation.

The term "whitepaper" originates from British government and was later adopted to describe a type of corporate marketing document. But where does the cryptocurrency community's special attachment to the term come from? Its origin goes back to Bitcoin, naturally. In October 2008, a pseudonymous author known as Satoshi Nakamoto published a nine-page text with the title "Bitcoin: A Peer-to-Peer Electronic Cash System."[11] This document became known as the Bitcoin whitepaper.

Its structure resembles a less formal version of a scientific research paper. As such there it begins with an abstract and has a list of references at the end, but the text itself clearly strives to be widely understandable by preferring illustrations to math or software code—there are only a handful of equations and one short piece of C code, which is not part of the Bitcoin implementation, but rather serves to illustrate a math concept to programmers.

The Bitcoin whitepaper is an admirable piece of tech writing because it strikes an efficient balance between scientific rigor and popular readability. It's therefore no wonder that it has inspired a generation of token designers who dream of having the next hot whitepaper.

Along the way, the example set by the Bitcoin whitepaper has been mangled practically beyond recognition. At one end, we now have whitepapers that are very long and technical, closer in structure to a traditional research paper rather than the short-form readability of Bitcoin's whitepaper. At the other end, we have whitepapers that have shed all pretense of being "papers" in the scientific sense and instead have become full-fledged PowerPoint pitch decks. It's a peculiar feature of the community that these two essentially unrelated types of documents are both still being called whitepapers. There is an element of "cargo cult" mentality at play: if you were honest and simply called your ICO presentation a pitch deck, it might give the impression that your project isn't a serious cryptocurrency protocol—so better call it a whitepaper like everyone else.

Some authors of protocols and token economy models have taken to providing multiple documents for different audiences: in addition to a technically oriented whitepaper, there may be a marketing-focused **color paper**, which is closer to a pitch deck. One simple way to draw the line between the two is the document's page format. A portrait-format document designed in a word processor that has an

---

[11] http://nakamotoinstitute.org/bitcoin

abstract at the top and contains mostly text is a whitepaper. A landscape-format document designed in PowerPoint or Keynote that has colorful logos and fancy charts showing skyrocketing token prices is a color paper.

Incidentally, fancy charts showing predicted token price evolution is a major bullshit indicator. Anyone who promises you guaranteed returns on any kind of investment is either hopelessly optimistic and deluded or an outright fraud. Either way, you don't want to necessarily invest in such people. Some ICOs of 2017 and 2018 attempted to blur the line by having complex sale structures, where the price keeps increasing during a month's-long sale process, thereby giving the promoters grounds to pretend that early investors will get an immediate return on their investment. But remember that it's not a profitable investment just because someone else bought the same thing for a higher price than you did. If there's no one to eventually buy the thing from you, it's worth exactly nothing.

For that reason, steer clear of the siren calls of ICO presale pricing schemes. *"Hurry, this price only valid for the next 24 hours!"* is the language of a hustler who's trying to make you buy something without giving it enough consideration. Instead, take your time and actually read the whitepaper. If you do that, you'll be better informed than 98 percent of people who invest in cryptocurrencies—and because investing is all about making informed decisions, you're almost guaranteed to be a better investor for it.

Before investing in any kind of new protocol or token, there are some fundamental questions that should be answered to your satisfaction. They are as follows:

### *Who are they?*

1. What's the background of the founders and other team members?
2. Do their credentials check out?
3. Does their track record indicate that they're truly capable of doing what they're promising?

### *Where does the money go?*

1. What's the legal structure behind this token or protocol?
2. Is there a company or foundation administering the funds?
3. Where is it registered?

4.  Who controls it?
5.  Does the project have sufficient investor vetting (KYC/AML) to satisfy regulations?

## *What are the guarantees?*

1.  Is there a smart contract in place that provides a blockchain-based token immediately when the ICO completes?
2.  Is the token the "real thing" promised by the team or just a placeholder that would be exchanged later when their technology hopefully is up and running?
3.  If the token is the final one, does it have immediate utility, or is that still years away?
4.  If the token has "distributed organization" type benefits like voting, are those features operational?

## *How likely is it that this will be a liquid asset?*

1.  Will the token be listed on an exchange so that you can sell it?
2.  Does the token have a utility function that would make someone other than speculators buy it? If so, when will there be substantial numbers of such users buying aftermarket tokens?

## *What future events can increase the token's value?*

1.  Does the ICO define artificial events like "token burning" that will reduce the number of tokens in the future, thus theoretically increasing the value of remaining tokens?
2.  What kind of partnerships and customer usage levels are required to make the token more valuable over time?

## *What's the level of technological readiness?*

1.  How much of the project's promised technology is up and running?
2.  Can the token be used for something already?
3.  If the team is promising a custom blockchain protocol or something similarly complex, do they have the necessary computer science competence and credible advisors?

### *Why is this project using blockchain technology?*

1. Is the use of a blockchain fundamental to the project somehow, or is it merely tacked on to capitalize on the ICO hype?
2. Does the project's implementation use the same blockchain where they're collecting funds? If not, why not?

### *Can the project reach its target market and partnerships?*

1. Where do the team members physically live? Can they easily access the market they're claiming to target?
2. How likely is it that the team can close partnership deals required to make the token useful?
3. What incentives does the token provide to third-party partners? Are they realistic?
4. Does the project have working partner integrations already? If not, when can those be expected?

### *Are the founders focused on their own wealth?*

1. How are the initial tokens allocated between team members, advisors, and external investors?
2. Are the funds going to be used to pay large salaries or other fees?
3. Do you have any way of following up to find out how the funds are actually being used?

If you can't easily find out the answers to these questions from reading a whitepaper and browsing the project's site, don't hesitate to contact the team. Practically all blockchain-based projects run a public chat room on Telegram, Slack, or something similar. Asking questions is a good way to judge the attitude and competence of team members. If they're evasive about basic questions such as the legal structure behind the project and which jurisdiction it's registered in, that's a major red flag.

For technology questions, the quality of answers may be harder to evaluate. The blockchain space is notorious for tech proposals that are extremely divisive, even among experts. Doing your own research on social media can be particularly difficult because many cryptocurrency projects have fervent supporter armies who will try to drown any criticism under a barrage of personal attacks. (IOTA is particularly notorious in this respect, but hardly the only one.) On the other hand, there's something of a blind spot on the other side as well: some technology experts have an axe to grind with all blockchain-based projects because they're fed up with the relentless hype from cryptocurrency promoters. You should be prepared to do a lot of reading to understand a protocol and the tradeoffs it makes. If you feel you're out of your depth in evaluating technology promises, it's generally best to err on the side of skepticism.

# 13.

# The Next Frontier for Blockchain: User Experience

Take a few dozen cryptocurrency experts and pundits and ask them what they think are the top challenges facing blockchain technology's adoption over the next few years, then compile a list of the most often mentioned challenges. Chances are that security and usability will be somewhere near the top of the list. There's widespread agreement that cryptocurrencies cleared a major hurdle in 2017 by becoming a category of investment that's being taken seriously, even on Wall Street—though certainly not institutionally. At the same time, a rapidly growing level of investment in blockchain technologies from major potential users like financial institutions and global technology consultants such as IBM has opened many doors for adoption. Yet all that has still been the easy part: now is the time to deliver on all that built-up interest.

Security remains a huge challenge because it's still rather poorly understood. Many of the strategies that have traditionally been used to manage and mitigate security risks in information technology rely on human judgment to identify security problems and manual effort to validate and verify access and transactions. These approaches don't work on blockchains: you can't have a person in the loop when the whole point is to have a global consensus algorithm making automatic decisions. A smart contract that defers judgment to a human could no longer be defined as such; it would no longer be inherently smart. Additionally, a broken smart contract can't be fixed by a human when it's revealed to be deficient. Lack of understanding about security risks and insufficiently robust programming practices have already led to hundreds of millions of dollars' worth of funds being stolen from Ethereum smart contracts. A single bug in a wallet's code in 2017 resulted in theft of $30 million worth of ETH[12]. Practices have been slow to improve: in June 2019, a team of researchers found easily-discovered exploits in real smart contracts that could expose $4 million of ETH[13].

Security is a major unresolved pain point for investors. If you have a million dollars in the bank, it's generally safe to expect that there are enough safeguards that your money can't be wired away by someone wearing sunglasses pretending to be you. But when that million is held in cryptocurrency, it can be silently and irrevocably stolen by anyone around the world who gains access to your private key—which is just a piece of text, easily exposed. Safely storing keys can become a matter of obsession to a cryptocurrency investor. Read Bitcoin-centric Twitter accounts for a while, and you'll inevitably see someone post pictures of USB keys with guns. Such a Wild West solution to securing one's money may seem workable in rural America, but it's not practical for most people around the world. To make cryptocurrency useful, better wallets are needed.

The other major challenge is usability. This is actually an area where great progress has already been made—it's just that, almost overwhelmingly, much remains to be done to enable the vision of blockchain-based "dApps" in use by the general public. Looking back some eight years to Bitcoin's initial stages,

---

[12] https://qz.com/1034321/ethereum-hack-a-coding-error-led-to-30-million-in-ethereum-being-stolen/

[13] https://www.investopedia.com/news/ethereum-smart-contracts-vulnerable-hacks-4-million-ether-risk/

usability was on the level of UNIX system administration tools: you needed to be proficient in running esoteric command-line programs to acquire coins and transfer them. A regular investor had no easy way of purchasing Bitcoin. Today, they can sign up on Coinbase, send some personal documentation, and in less than 24 hours be up and running trading cryptocurrencies using a friendly smartphone app.

Security and usability come together under the more generic umbrella of **user experience**, usually abbreviated as **UX**. The domain of UX is simply everything that affects how the user perceives a digital product and interacts with it. Coinbase is a shining example of successful UX in this space. It's not just about having a nice smartphone app: a crucial part of the Coinbase UX is that they provided credible and easily understandable security in an environment tainted by catastrophic failures of other exchanges, like the MtGox bankruptcy. Coinbase has been a UX breakthrough for one group of blockchain stakeholders—individual investors looking to dip their toe into cryptocurrency. To deliver on promises made by protocols, similar UX breakthroughs will need to happen for other stakeholders, too. This includes customers who want to make payments in cryptocurrency, sellers who want to easily receive money, regular end users who might use a dApp instead of a centralized web app, and also the developers themselves. The current state of smart contract development tools is not good enough because simple programming mistakes can lead to latent bugs that lose customer funds years later. Creators of dApps will need better UX, or they won't be able to deliver the secure and usable solutions sought by users.

The lack of truly easy-to-use cryptocurrency solutions for buyers and sellers is an acute pain point that has been somewhat masked by the enormous success of Bitcoin and Ethereum as speculative investments. If you recall from Chapter 13, the 2008 Bitcoin whitepaper's title was, "A peer-to-peer electronic cash system." Clearly Bitcoin hasn't delivered on this original promise of being a system for small transactions. Nobody would pretend that Bitcoin at its present market cap and constrained transaction volume is suitable for cash-like use—it's not reasonable to pay for a cup of coffee with a currency that can fluctuate 10 percent in a day and imposes multi-dollar fees on small purchases.

There are several well-funded and competent teams working to fix this UX problem for various blockchains. The Lightning Network is currently the most advanced candidate for a genuine cash-like payment system backed by Bitcoin. Once the protocol works, there remains the question of payment UX. Who's going to make a truly easy-to-use wallet for mobile payments using Lightning, or whatever emerges as the winning micro-transaction protocol? What company will provide vendors with a globally accessible software solution that makes it easier and cheaper to accept cryptocurrency than credit cards? Those will be necessary cornerstones of a payment UX revolution.

It's not going to be easy to deliver on the promise of micro-scale blockchain payments for a global user base. The original dream of cash-like cryptocurrencies has been an elusive chimera so far, but perhaps the stars are aligning. The ascendancy of Bitcoin as a store of value gives it a degree of credibility that didn't exist in 2008, and investment in technologies like Lightning may crack the hard, technical challenges. Ultimately, adoption may depend on larger economic trends: if faith in fiat currencies falters for whatever reason, the volatility of cryptocurrencies may not seem so bad in comparison.

Distributed apps looking to use smart contracts for applications outside of payment transactions face an even more difficult uphill battle to gain user adoption. The user experience is simply abysmal at present. There are startups building things like decentralized Twitter clones on the Ethereum blockchain, but it's not remotely credible that anyone would start using such a thing when sending a message costs real money, and anyone who wants to follow you would have to install a flaky browser plugin that connects to Ethereum, then takes 30 minutes just to get started because it needs to sync with the blockchain. As the saying goes, there's no "there" there for these dApps. The current performance and capacity of the Ethereum blockchain just doesn't make sense for any applications outside of those that move relatively large amounts of money in relatively few transactions. Crowdsale escrows (ICOs) and "cryptokitties" are working examples of such, but even they have already managed to strain Ethereum's transaction limits to a breaking point.

Ethereum may yet become the promised dApp platform thanks to ongoing technical developments like sharding; or perhaps a different blockchain design like EOSIO ends up being a more workable solution. Blockchain-aware browsers like Brave may be the answer to acute usability issues of how users interact with dApps. Yet one aspect of the dApp UX quandary remains unaddressed: how will developers create better, more reliable apps? We've already seen that old software development methods aren't delivering when it comes to smart contracts. Rapid-iteration methodologies, like **Agile Development**, and slogans like Facebook's famous "Move Fast and Break Things" are the opposite of what's needed to create robust software on blockchains.

The bar has been raised much higher than ever before. Creating high-usability dApps will still require user-centric iteration, just like in the world of centralized software. But something needs to happen to make sure that the solutions delivered at the end of the iterative process are stable and verified.

Thanks in part to ICOs, there are now many well-funded teams working on improving the development experience. Some focus on fundamental protocol issues by integrating verified software design methodologies similar to those used by mission-critical systems design (think airplanes and spacecraft); others are building one-click tools for smart contract deployment. Yet they all share a common goal. The UX revolution needs to be embraced by developers first, otherwise dApps can never be good enough to maintain user trust.

If developer tools are only now being designed, genuine end-user applications must be years away. Yet there are positive effects that can be felt much sooner. During the so-called "Web 2.0 revolution," the pendulum of software design trends had swung far towards highly centralized applications. The interest in blockchains has sparked new ways of thinking about decentralization as a core principle. Similarly, the integration of cryptocurrency tokens into software has unleashed a new awareness of economies in software. Developers are now thinking actively of how users and other stakeholders can work together to unlock the benefits of a software platform and the software protocols that connect its participants. In Web 2.0, the default answer to economic questions was basically: "We'll sell ads once we have enough people on our platform," a fine answer for some platforms, but ultimately very limiting for innovation. Everybody working in software should be thankful to Bitcoin and smart contracts for showing an alternate path, even if the ultimate end-user realization of the vision might end up being nothing like what 2017's high-flying ICOs imagined.

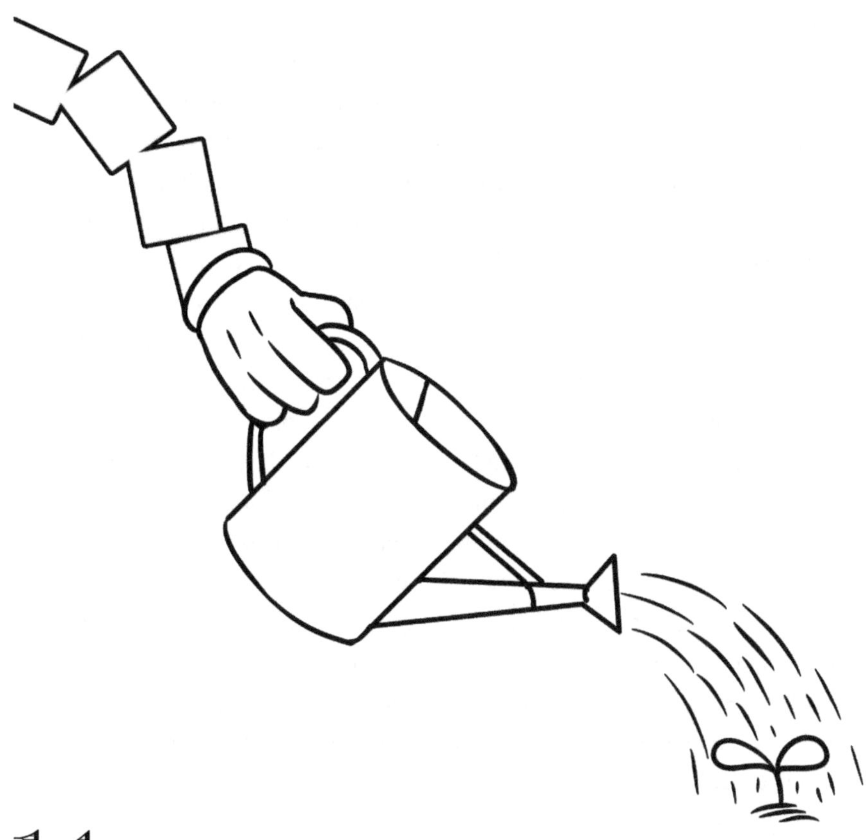

# 14.

# Innovative Applications for Blockchain: Social Impact

An exciting new development in blockchain technology is the realization of its many applications for good. As the "tech for good" community takes on innovative applications of machine learning, AI, and even basic data analytics, there is a space for blockchain to address some basic needs within the social impact space.

There are a variety of ways in which blockchain can be used toward providing resources for humanitarian efforts, addressing systemic challenges to global equity (financial and otherwise) and beyond. The possibilities are vast, and it is important to continue to invest in research and development within this space.

There are some notable examples of "blockchain for good" uses that have been left out of the above section at this time as more work is needed before they can be validated as viable opportunities. For example, while expanded access to voting is imperative in our modern democratic system, there are some concerns with the present solution: mobile voting with the app Voatz[14]. While it is beyond the scope of this book to suggest improvements or alternative solutions, we encourage you to read more about dissenting opinions[15,16] on the use of this app, or even electronic voting more broadly. One thing is clear, however: individuals in poor communities of color are often disenfranchised from exercising their right to vote, and any solution that securely addresses this inequity would be welcome.

Back to a brighter note, there are many organizations doing "blockchain for good" extremely well. The World Food Programme cites the reduced overhead and security of blockchain as two of its primary reasons for using this technology to feed more hungry individuals. They indicate that using blockchain yields a "faster intervention in some of the world's most difficult operating environments."[17] Their "Building Blocks" project, utilizing Ethereum as its currency, enables the agency to validate and create a record of cash and in-kind transactions without the need for traditional government identification. This addresses a key problem cited earlier in the book and holds the potential for additional humanitarian efforts, particularly with refugees and displaced individuals.

No credit is (just) one significant barrier to financial inclusion. Many of the world's poorest are without access to bank accounts, credit, and other financial tools. When an individual lacks a credit history, they are unable to avail themselves of these and many other wealth benefits. By including activities that are non-traditionally considered credit-building in the composition of an individual's "economic footprint," a person is empowered to gain access to banking and other financial benefits[18]. BankQu[19] is one such platform.

---

[14] https://www.theverge.com/2018/11/10/18080518/blockchain-voting-mobile-app-west-virginia-voatz

[15] https://techcrunch.com/2018/08/11/voatz-a-tale-of-a-terrible-horrible-no-good-very-bad-idea/

[16] https://www.vanityfair.com/news/2018/08/smartphone-voting-is-coming-just-in-time-for-midterms-voatz

[17] https://innovation.wfp.org/blog/blockchain-crypto-assistance-wfp

[18] http://pubdocs.worldbank.org/en/710961476811913780/Session-5C-Pani-Baruri-Block-chain-Financial-Inclusion-Pani.pdf

[19] https://banqu.co/

# Conclusion

We hope that you have found the contents of this book useful. Blockchain technology holds the potential to advance industry that has been stagnant for quite some time. We encourage you to approach cryptocurrency with the careful optimism that we do and to do your research thoroughly before investing. Happy blockchaining!

# Index